LEARNING EXPERIENCES IN SCHOOL RENEWAL

AN EXPLORATION OF FIVE SUCCESSFUL PROGRAMS

EDITED BY

BRUCE JOYCE AND EMILY CALHOUN

Clearinghouse on Educational Management

University of Oregon

1996

Library of Congress Cataloging-in-Publication Data

Learning experiences in school renewal : an exploration of five successful programs / edited by Bruce Joyce and Emily Calhoun.
        p.   cm.
    Includes bibliographical references (p.   ).
    ISBN 0-86552-133-6
    1.   School improvement programs—United States—Case studies.
    2.   Action research in education—United States—Case studies.
    I. Joyce, Bruce R.   II. Calhoun, Emily.   III.   ERIC Clearinghouse on Educational Management.
    LB2822.82.L43 1996
    371.2'00973—dc20   96-22596
                                                             CIP

Printed in the United States of America, 1996

Design: LeeAnn August
Type: 11/12.5 Times
Printer: BookCrafters, Chelsea, Michigan (118269)

ERIC Clearinghouse on Educational Management
    5207 University of Oregon
    Eugene, OR   97403-5207
    Telephone: (541) 346-5043   Fax: (541) 346-2334
ERIC/CEM Accession Number: EA 026 696

This publication was prepared in part with funding from the Office of Educational Research and Improvement, U.S. Department of Education, under contract no. OERI-RR 93002006. The opinions expressed in this report do not necessarily reflect the positions or policies of the Department of Education. No federal funds were used in the printing of this publication.

The University of Oregon is an equal opportunity, affirmative action institution committed to cultural diversity.

MISSION OF ERIC
AND THE CLEARINGHOUSE

The Educational Resources Information Center (ERIC) is a national information system operated by the U.S. Department of Education. ERIC serves the educational community by disseminating research results and other resource information that can be used in developing more effective educational programs.

The ERIC Clearinghouse on Educational Management, one of several such units in the system, was established at the University of Oregon in 1966. The Clearinghouse and its companion units process research reports and journal articles for announcement in ERIC's index and abstract bulletins.

Research reports are announced in *Resources in Education* (*RIE*), available in many libraries and by subscription from the United States Government Printing Office, Washington, D.C. 20402-9371.

Most of the documents listed in *RIE* can be purchased through the ERIC Document Reproduction Service, operated by Cincinnati Bell Information Systems.

Journal articles are announced in *Current Index to Journals in Education. CIJE* is also available in many libraries and can be ordered from Oryx Press, 4041 North Central Avenue at Indian School, Suite 700, Phoenix, Arizona 85012. Semiannual cumulations can be ordered separately.

Besides processing documents and journal articles, the Clearinghouse prepares bibliographies, literature reviews, monographs, and other interpretive research studies on topics in its educational area.

CLEARINGHOUSE
NATIONAL ADVISORY BOARD

George Babigian, Executive Director, American Education Finance Association
Anne L. Bryant, Executive Director, National School Boards Association
Esther Coleman, Executive Director, American Association of School Personnel
    Administrators
Timothy J. Dyer, Executive Director, National Association of Secondary School
    Principals
Patrick Forsyth, Executive Director, University Council for Educational
    Administration
Paul Houston, Executive Director, American Association of School Administrators
Joyce G. McCray, Executive Director, Council for American Private Education
Samuel G. Sava, Executive Director, National Association of Elementary School
    Principals
Gail T. Schneider, Vice-President, Division A, American Educational Research
    Association
Don I. Tharpe, Executive Director, Association of School Business Officials
    International
Brenda Welburn, Executive Director, National Association of State Boards of
    Education

ADMINISTRATIVE STAFF

Philip K. Piele, Professor and Director
Stuart C. Smith, Associate Director for Publications

CONTENTS

FOREWORD

These five case studies of school systems that made serious attempts to become true learning communities report both effects on student learning and lessons for others having similar goals in the future. If carefully read and discussed, the cases will provide valuable insights for others seeking to transform institutions into places where parents, faculties, and students continually learn about learning.

No one really knows what will be the future of public education in a society where only about half the parents rate the school their child attends as excellent or good. Politicians are generating symbolic legislation by authorizing "charter" schools. Many politicians openly support "vouchers" and the privatization of education despite the dubious constitutionality of those proposals.

Attempts to legislate school improvement and attempts by local school boards to improve standards both indicate how much education has become a high-stakes concern in our society. Real school improvement will not come about through legislation or even state or local "standards" for excellence in schooling. School renewal will come about by sustained local work of the type vividly described in the case studies reported here. We can't just tell people to do a better job, we have to roll up our sleeves and create a workplace where school improvement is the norm. Today's schools look remarkably like they did 50 years ago. Years of criticism and rhetoric have not improved them.

The lessons from these successful programs make clear that the culture of schools must change to where learning is the central focus of a *workplace*. In that workplace, the search for more powerful teaching strategies is embedded in ongoing staff development designed well enough that real change in curriculum and instruction takes place under governance structures that move schools toward democratic practices in which workers and clients have direct responsibility for improvement. These cultural changes parallel the revolution in private-sector organizations where continuous training, collective decision-making, and worker responsibility are intertwined.

Readers will appreciate that cases range from small to large school districts in several regions of the country and in a DoDDS region. They will also appreciate the many types of data reported: interviews, surveys, observations, studies of changes in governance and teaching, and several types of measures of student learning.

In several of the cases, teachers learned teaching strategies that few teachers have available to them in most districts today, and the results affirm the recent research on staff development that shows that well-designed training enables most teachers to learn strategies that are new to them.

The reports include many things that didn't go well, including the skepticism of many teachers and administrators, lack of central organization support in some settings (and outstanding support in others), problems of communication about purpose, and the common initial belief that new practices "won't work with my kids."

Staff development was critical and, in several of the cases, resulted in above-average implementation with consequent effects on student learning. In action research, the staff development is in the form of technical assistance both in the process of action research and in the organizational changes needed to permit action research to flourish. Even so, schools need to adopt curricular and instructional changes and generate the staff development necessary for those changes to move from intent to reality.

We need to take action that is informed by the knowledge base on curriculum and teaching that now exists, and at the same time we need to continually expand that knowledge base. The question is whether student performance significantly increases when we enable teachers and administrators to learn and use this knowledge base. The answer provided in these cases is clearly affirmative. If we don't find ways to make schools true learning communities that rely on and expand the knowledge base, we are destined for more short-term tinkering and legislated requirements as well as flat or even declining student performance with respect to the knowledge and skills they need for the future.

The spirit of these case studies provides an affirmative message. We *can* make the needed changes in curriculum and instruction, and, capitalizing on knowledge about how to influence the culture of the schools, we can do so in a way that can change schools into learning organizations.

Gordon Cawelti
Project Director
Alliance for Curriculum Reform
Arlington, Virginia

ACKNOWLEDGMENTS

All the authors give thanks to the truly enormous number of colleagues who made these learning experiences happen. In fact, the learning happened because everyone in the associated schools or districts participated.

More than 3,000 teachers and administrators were directly involved, and the projects were intended to improve the education of somewhere around 60,000 students. Many parents helped in ways large and small and were extremely supportive; there were virtually no instances of the parent/community turmoil that innovation occasions in so many settings these days. Similarly, the boards of education played their part, in some cases displaying real courage as they backed educational reform by approving unusual arrangements for staff development, assessment, and governance, and persuading their communities to foot the bill.

The top administrators were marvelous. In our times, leaders can become controversial for pressing for reform of the type carried on in these relentless programs, and can even be sacrificed for being the proverbial messenger. These folks walked out front.

These reports are the product of true participatory research. Although experienced researchers were involved, virtually everyone collected data, helped organize it, and worried over it. Inevitably, the participants were the subjects of their own research.

The design both of the programs and their accompanying research hinged on the efforts of a long line of social and behavioral scientists. The great scholars of curriculum and instruction, action research, training, change, and organizational development were there with us, for the knowledge base of the field was alive in these designs. Equal to our gratitude for the knowledge and tools of these scholars is our appreciation for their spirit of inquiry, their belief that disciplined study is possible in field settings, and their insight that field research may be the central avenue for the development of knowledge in an area like school renewal.

CHAPTER 1

LEARNING-CENTERED SCHOOL RENEWAL

BRUCE JOYCE AND EMILY CALHOUN

The search for better strategies for school renewal is the theme. This book reports five case studies, each of which took the form of action research into the school-renewal process over periods of from three to five years. Technical and social aspects of school renewal were examined in each program as district personnel and school faculties sought to learn how to build learning communities for adults and children alike.

The settings are different, as are the designs of the programs, but the inquiry mode that dominated their efforts binds the five. Breadth of involvement and leadership were structured into each program. Extensive technical support for their efforts was available from the beginning, from inside and outside the district and schools. In four settings, all teachers and administrators in the schools or districts participated in extensive staff development and/or community-building activities. In each case, formative evaluation or action research was used to assess implementation, effects on students, and the response of the social system and the organization.

THE PROGRAMS

Geographically, the programs occurred in the Southeast, Midwest, Far West, and an overseas region of the Department of Defense Dependents Schools. The real names of the cities and towns are not given to permit candor in describing organizational problems while reducing the probability that the brave, hard-working project personnel will be liable to criticism.

THE RIVER CITY PROGRAM

In what seemed to be a major innovation eight years ago, whole schools joined, by majority vote, an intensive school-renewal program. These faculties committed themselves to a collegial organization, the intensive study of teaching and curriculum, the formative study of student learning, and the study of implementation.

THE UNIVERSITY TOWN PROGRAM

This program was structured around individual, school (through action research), and district levels of staff development. The University Town program illustrates many of the features of the school as a center of inquiry—embedded time for colleagueship; a system for shared decision-making; an information-rich, formative study environment; the study of research on curriculum and teaching; and a comprehensive staff development system that includes study groups. Formative studies of teacher satisfaction, implementation, and effects on students permitted an investigation of the productivity of individual, school, and district governance.

THE READERSVILLE PROGRAM

This program was designed to build a culture of readers. All the teachers, administrators, parents, and children of a district of 11 schools were involved in an "at home" reading program conducted as action research by the entire community. At-home reading of all the students was studied intensively, including effects on quality of writing and on the results from standard tests of reading.

THE INNER CITY PROGRAM

The Inner City Initiative for School Improvement was designed to provide excellence in student learning and in the workplace of educational professionals. With respect to the students, the intent was to ensure that no student be disadvantaged educationally, regardless of conditions in the home. Goals were to ensure normal or above-average growth in personal qualities, social skills, values, citizenship, and academic work. With respect to teachers and administrators, the intent was to build a self-renewing organization where innovative collegiality and the study of teaching and curriculum are the norm.

THE ACTION NETWORK: ACTION RESEARCH ON ACTION RESEARCH

In a Southeastern state, the faculties of 60 schools worked to build shared governance and generate schoolwide action research. Technical assistance was provided to leadership teams through workshops, an information-retrieval system, and a yearly on-site visit. For five years, the progress of schools in Action Network has been studied through action research. The dynamics of the most successful schools have been identified. Based on these studies, technical assistance has been improved and brought to the point where schools wishing to adopt the action-research paradigm can implement it more rapidly and effectively.

PROGRAMMATIC SIMILARITIES AND DIFFERENCES

The five programs we describe share three characteristics: the primary focus was improving student learning; the major school-improvement strategy was an investment in people; and each program was designed and conducted as a learning experience to generate knowledge about important aspects of school renewal and staff development. In four of the cases, initiatives were made to directly influence the learning of children, and implementation and effects on student learning were studied. In the fifth case, a strenuous effort was made to turn schools into self-renewing organizations through shared governance and action research, and the effects were studied in terms of changes in the professional community of 60 schools, the initiatives they generated, and their effects on students.

DEMOGRAPHIC DIFFERENCES

The River City Program was in a school district that served 30,000 students; its student achievement has traditionally been about the same as the average for the country.

The University Town Program is in a smaller district that served 5,000 students; its student achievement has traditionally placed it among the top 5 percent in the nation.

In Readersville the 11 schools of a Department of Defense Dependents Schools region studied the "at home" reading and the in-school and out-of-school writing of their students and generated a community program to increase reading and writing and study the effects of doing so.

The Inner City Program is in an urban school district of about 100 schools where student achievement has traditionally been among the poorest in the nation. Most of Inner City's 350,000 residents are caught in a vise of urban decay.

The Action Network brought together more than 60 schools with varied demographics scattered throughout a Southeastern state to generate shared governance built around the study of student learning.

SIMILARITIES IN SCHOOL-IMPROVEMENT APPROACHES

Each program used the formative study of implementation and effects on students to guide changes in the initiatives. In three programs, the core of staff development was designed around the theory-demonstration-practice-peer coaching paradigm developed from Joyce and Showers' research on how teachers add curricular and instructional models to their repertoires.

In all five programs, all teachers and administrators in the schools of focus were involved: 16 schools in River City, 9 elementary schools in University Town, 5 "demonstration schools" in Inner City, 11 schools in Readersville, and 60 schools in Action Network.

In three programs (River City, University Town, and Inner City), all the teachers studied several models of teaching. Peer-coaching teams were organized to support changes in all schools; implementation data were gathered and used to modulate training; and student learning was studied. These programs were designed to continue or to be succeeded by equally intensive projects; therefore, district and program organizers gave significant support to the schools, and cadres of teachers and administrators were prepared to support other schools and continue the study of teaching within the district.

GLEANINGS

Let us begin by considering a number of contemporary questions regarding the state of knowledge about education and the quest to improve schooling in America:

Is enough known about teaching, staff development, and school renewal to design programs with a high probability of success in raising student learning?

Can school-community programs be created that affect the home environment in ways that fit with the goals of the school and generate student behavior that raises achievement?

Is action research an effective paradigm for school renewal? How much help do schools need if they are to use it effectively?

Can staff development/school renewal be effectively governed by school districts, schools, and individuals? Are there differences that favor one level over another?

Can school renewal change the influence on future learning of gender, race, ethnicity, socioeconomic status, and prior achievement?

Is enough known about school renewal to bring about the cultural changes in the educational community to make self-renewing schools commonplace?

The case studies accumulated information that bears on the above questions and a number of others that are frequently asked. The cases do not provide definitive answers—they are part of the continuing inquiry into them. Nonetheless, they have generated findings that will confirm the opinions of some and challenge seriously some contemporary conventional wisdom.

Throughout the book, we try to make clear that the case studies are not reports of inventions to be packaged and transferred unceremoniously to other settings. True, they are descriptions of very large-scale improvement programs and their considerable effects on student learning. However, the essential story in each case is of a complex inquiry into aspects of the school-improvement process.

The information generated from these five cases illustrates the emergent nature of knowledge: contemporary school-renewal theories and programmatic assumptions are sometimes confirmed and sometimes challenged by the findings. Some puzzlements seem somewhat clearer whereas others are even more muddled. But the entire effort inches us along as we try to grapple with the kinds of questions outlined above.

KNOWLEDGE OF TEACHING AND SCHOOL RENEWAL

Is enough known about teaching, staff development, and school renewal to design programs with a high probability of success in raising student learning? A general test of educational theory.

In one sense, asking this question seems almost Alicelike. On one hand, isn't the obvious point of educational research and theory-building to support productive change? On the other hand, many practitioners and researchers question whether enough is known to *effectively* provide a basis for programs that will probably succeed. While only a few educators feel the knowledge base is completely empty, many wonder how full is the storehouse.

In 1993, an entire issue of the *Review of Educational Research* was devoted to arguments over whether there is a useful knowledge base about teaching—the core of educational activity. In the same year, *The Journal of Staff Development* included a section built around the assertion by some reviewers that there is no proven link between staff development and student learning. Without such a link, how can research be of earthly use in staff development and school-improvement programs?

Bev Showers puts it well when she says that the major import of the River City and University Town projects was that they are general tests of educational theory. Essentially, can programs be designed on the basis of a body of educational theory and research with a high probability that they will change the educational environment for a sustained period, generate increased student learning of a consider-able magnitude, and result in significant changes in collegiality? In River City and University Town, entire faculties of teachers (25 schools in all) studied heavily researched, theory-based models of teaching. These two studies followed a heavily researched staff development design created to bring about a high degree of imple-mentation of those models in the basic curriculum areas.

In both cases, the teaching models became a part of the active repertoire of the teachers, students learned to respond to the changes in curriculum and instruction, student achievement rose markedly according to multiple measures, and the collegial relationships among teachers and between teachers and administrators changed greatly.

A massive complex of initiatives was designed to impact student learning in Inner City. Importantly, although implementation was uneven, the schools were able to absorb the impact of the initiatives; the faculties were not fragile, though several were organizationally chaotic as the program began. Considerable increases in student learning occurred, again unevenly. However, the program demon-strated that school renewal can begin with substantial changes in curriculum and instruction provided that the initiatives include con-siderable amounts of staff development and technical assistance.

The results are direct evidence that there is enough in the store-house of educational theory and research to design school-renewal programs that will affect student achievement and collegiality. The finding concurs with the recent research by Slavin and his associates (1990, 1995), Sharan and Hertz-Lazarowitz and their colleagues (1982, 1988, 1990), Wallace and his team (1990), and a number of others.

Is this knowledge applicable in all settings? We think so. But would we expect completely equivalent results across all settings?

Probably not. For example, in the case of Inner City, an extremely troubled urban school district, some very positive results were achieved, but the culture of the central office was an impediment throughout, and the design team could not help them realize the full potential of the content of the program or understand how to institutionalize school renewal in the culture of the district.

HOME-SCHOOL RELATIONSHIP

Can school-community programs be created that affect the home environment in ways that fit with the goals of the school and generate student behavior that raises achievement? A test of capability to affect school-parent-community relations.

Again, at first reading, this appears to be another Alicelike question. On the one hand it appears obvious that schools can have such an influence and there are many examples of such. On the other, many practitioners complain that the family environments of children greatly impede or enhance learning but the schools are relatively helpless to change conditions in the home.

Readersville (chapter 4) implemented a districtwide action-research program called "Just Read" in which all the schools studied at-home reading by the students and created community efforts to increase at-home independent reading and writing. Parents, teachers, and students worked together to build a culture of readers and writers.

The Readersville program worked very well. The language arts curriculum followed the children into their living rooms. Amounts of "at-home" reading by all increased several-fold, and the "lowest readers" read books they selected independently at a rate several times what the average had been; the "highest" readers read about 10 times what the "highest" had read before. The socioeconomic status, ethnicity, race, and gender of the families were not factors in implementation.

Nor did demography influence increases in learning. Quality of writing improved dramatically across the board, though there was not a general curricular change beyond the extension of the language arts curriculum into the home, and scores of tests of reading comprehension rose substantially.

The Readersville results support the proposition that schools can affect "at home" behavior substantially and, in so doing, affect the academic environment of the school. Could "Just Read" be used in any community? We think so. It was used in the Inner City Program and in several other communities that differ widely—a largely Hispanic district near the Mexican border, a university town, an upscale suburban school district. Its effects were strongly influenced by the degree of leadership from principals and lead teachers. With respect to community involvement, it appears that where there is will, there are ways.

ACTION RESEARCH

Is action research an effective paradigm for school renewal? How much help do schools need if they are to use it effectively? A test of the general theory of action research.

As a formal theory, action research has been around for a good 60 years and is one of the major lines of thinking about "grass roots" renewal in business, industry, and schooling. Its popularity waned for a while but is glowing brightly at present. Yet, there is surprisingly little action research on action-research in education. The issue of whether building democratic, data-driven faculty environments will achieve its goals has been studied only tangentially. The action-research paradigm that was employed here includes (1) generating a degree of democratic governance in the school, (2) helping faculties study the health of the educational environment, (3) using those studies to make initiatives, (4) studying the effects, and (5) recycling the process (see chapter 6). Looking over the picture of the more than 70 schools whose stories are told in chapter 6, it appears that two conclusions are warranted:

1. Action research can work, and very effectively. Some schools did very well.
2. Probably all could have, had they had adequate technical assistance.

The difference between schools that tried to process their own way through the action-research paradigm and those that received help was dramatic. Furthermore, help was needed in all phases of the paradigm.

So, in answer to the question "Does the action-research paradigm bring about school renewal?," the import of these studies is "yes," provided that the process is accompanied by generous amounts of technical assistance. In other words, it appears at this time that most faculties are unable to teach themselves how to make the paradigm work. These results fit with research on other paradigms that are recommended for site-based and controlled school improvement. For example, the studies of the Coalition of Essential Schools, the State of California School Improvement Programs, and several others have indicated that most of their schools are stalled.

The studies on the Action Network reported in chapter 6 indicated that many school faculties appear to have a much easier time generating initiatives for school improvement than learning how to collect and share data about the health of the school, generate initiatives based on those data, and then collect information to track those initiatives, assess effects, and modulate the initiatives accordingly.

The development of democratic process and the use of data-based processes for school improvement are apparently more foreign to the culture of school faculties than is the making of initiatives based on perceptions. However, based on studies of the Action Network, improvements in technical assistance bring action research into the culture of schools more rapidly and effectively than was the case just a few years ago.

GOVERNANCE ISSUES

Can staff development/school renewal be effectively governed by school districts, schools, and individuals? Are there differences that favor one level over another? Are their differences in the satisfaction and productivity when staff development is governed by individuals, faculties, or district offices?

For about 20 years there has been a more or less continuous and sometimes vehement debate about the most effective ways of governing staff development, particularly whether individuals, faculties, districts, or some combination should be the governors. Some argue passionately that only individuals can know their personal needs and choose how to study (Elliott 1991, Hollingsworth and Sockett 1994). Others center on the school (Barth 1990, Glickman 1993), and many policy-makers have elected the "site-based" option. Curriculum planners tend to focus on the role of the district to generate equity in curriculum and instruction.

In University Town (chapter 3), the district provided handsome support to staff development governed at all three levels of the organization, providing a comparative perspective for what we believe is the first time.

The results indicate that governance by individuals, schools, or districts can work, but it was harder to get the individual and school levels working than the district level. The results are directly contradictory to those who argue that district planners are doomed to failure because their plans cannot gain acceptance by teachers and building administrators. The results are also cautionary. As in the case of Action Network (chapter 6), faculty-centered efforts required substantial technical assistance. And many individuals were simply at a loss to generate their own activities, even when supported by as much as $1,000 in a given year.

STUDENT CHARACTERISTICS

Can school renewal influence student learning more powerfully than stereotypic predictors such as gender, race, ethnicity, socioeconomic status, and prior achievement?

One of the most important issues with respect to the power of educational treatments involves the interaction of any treatment with the characteristics of the students. The magnitude of the issue derives from the fact that with most common treatments (how education is usually carried on) demographic differences have a very large effect, producing huge disequities in educational opportunity. Thus, if a treatment is generated from research, an automatic question needs to be: "How does it interact with gender, ethnicity, race, socioeconomic status, and the student's learning history (previous achievement) to date?"

The overall message from these case studies is quite positive. In River City, a middle school that served only black students raised its promotion rate from 30 percent to over 90 percent, with changes in norm-referenced test scores to match. Inner City had more uneven implementation but some similar results overall. In Readersville, results were independent of any demographic factors. In University Town, a traditionally high-achieving district, gender differences in competence in writing were reduced considerably.

A dream of educators has always been to be effective enough to raise student achievement not just for some, but for all, making educational inequity a thing of the past. These cases provide one more matrix of information that the right kind of treatment can approach that goal.

CULTURES OF RENEWAL

Is enough known about school renewal to bring about the cultural changes in the educational community to make self-renewing schools commonplace?

This question can be addressed in two ways. One is the subquestion "How long does it take to bring about the collaborative conditions that make major school-improvement initiatives possible?" The other is "How long does it take to institutionalize collaborative inquiry so that the school is in a state of perpetual school renewal?"

With respect to the first question, the answer is "not long." In every case, teachers and administrators coalesced to bring about increases in student learning within the first year of the inception of the programs. With respect to the second question—the time it takes for renewal to become self-perpetuating—the information leads to considerable ambiguity. Although changes in the workplace have been sustained for several years and the orientation toward school renewal has weathered many storms in each case, they still appear to be person-dependent to the degree that they will gradually disappear over time as the key personnel leave. A great deal of research is needed in this area.

SOME OTHER FREQUENTLY ASKED QUESTIONS

The embedded studies provided information about several other questions that refine and sharpen inquiries in the staff-development and school-renewal fields.

Do the age and experience of educators influence their motivation?

Frequently, questions are raised about the influence of age and experience on the motivation of teachers and administrators to engage enthusiastically in school-improvement programs. Often, it is suggested that age and experience reduce motivation. Age and experience as factors were addressed directly in the River City, University Town, and Readersville programs. In all cases, they were not factors. Motivation does not appear to be related to age or experience. If anything, age and experience increase receptivity to innovations.

Is the dynamic of school renewal influenced by the demographic characteristics of the schools or school districts?

The cases involve school-improvement efforts in school districts that varied widely. The problems, obstacles, and issues of organization were very similar.

Do the demographic differences among school districts require different curricular and instructional approaches?

In these cases, demography did not influence the effectiveness of educational treatments within or between programs.

SUMMARY

The stories will unfold in the chapters that follow. The reader is urged to follow the stories not as attempts to "prove" that particular school-improvement efforts "work," but rather to see them as part of our struggle to contribute knowledge to the slowly emerging field of school improvement.

RIVER CITY

In what seemed to be a major innovation eight years ago, whole schools joined, by majority vote, an intensive school-renewal program. These faculties committed themselves to a collegial organization, the intensive study of teaching and curriculum, and the formative study of implementation and student learning.

A cadre of teachers disseminated the program to 16 schools, demonstrating the ability of teachers to transport a multidimensional program to faculties where all members participate.

The most dramatic instance of student learning was in a middle school where the promotion rate rose from 30 percent to 90 percent in two years, an effect that has been sustained for six more years

CHAPTER 2

THE RIVER CITY PROGRAM: STAFF DEVELOPMENT BECOMES SCHOOL IMPROVEMENT

BEVERLY SHOWERS, CARLENE MURPHY, AND BRUCE JOYCE

> What happens when entire school faculties engage in the study of teaching and school improvement?

We visit a program where the faculties of three schools joined in an effort to improve the performance of their schools. Several other noteworthy features also distinguished this three-year program: Models of teaching were the content, the classic training paradigm was used, formative evaluation of implementation and effects on students was embedded, a cadre of teachers learned to disseminate the program, and the procedures were shaped to increase self-renewing capability by school faculties.

We use this inquiry into school improvement to investigate technical questions about the transmission of teaching skills to a large number of teachers, the preparation and effectiveness of the cadre, and the link between implementation and student learning. And we use it to investigate social questions about the participation of faculties as a whole, the reception of the program by the district organization, the creation of self-renewing capacity, and the social-psychological reactions of teachers and administrators.

SETTING AND CONTEXT

The River City program (called locally the "MOT Program" (for Models of Teaching) is situated in a County School District in a Southeastern state. A city of about 50,000 people is the commercial center of the county, which houses about 200,000 people overall. The metropolitan area extends into an adjacent county of largely affluent suburbs, and also reaches into the edge of a neighboring state. In 54 schools, 1,800 teachers and about 800 teaching assistants serve about 33,000 children. Economic prosperity varies widely. About 60 percent of the students qualify for free or reduced lunch. The largest employers are a military installation, a medical college, and a high-tech factory that produces plutonium. A division of the state higher education system is located there. African-Americans and Caucasians each make up about half of the population.

STUDENT ACHIEVEMENT AND "AT RISK" PROGRAMS

For years before MOT was initiated in the 1987-88 school year, teachers, parents, and administrators had been frustrated by the low levels of achievement of many students. In percentile terms, measured by the Iowa test battery, mean achievement in the major curriculum areas hung in the 40s and, in some schools, in the 20s and 30s. Even without the use of the standard test battery, it would have been apparent that achievement left something to be desired, because teachers and administrators knew that a third of the students were not learning to read independently, many dropped out during the middle and high school years, and few students were outstanding.

In addition, energy spent on disciplinary action was considerable. Throughout the district, from 20 to 30 percent of the middle and high school students were suspended in any given year, and the situation for elementary schools was not much better. In one elementary school, the percent suspended regularly reached 20.

The district, although not affluent (the per pupil expenditure based on average daily attendance figures was less than $3,000 from all sources), was very active in the use of a variety of initiatives designed to improve student learning, particularly ones to help students identified as "at risk." Some of these activities were subsidized by state and federal sources, as in the case of Title I (then called Chapter 1) and special-education programs, but others were created by the district itself. Eight hundred paid instructional aides worked in nearly half of the classrooms. Curriculum was updated regularly, and staff development was offered for teachers and administrators.

Despite these efforts, many students remained in academic difficulty. To illustrate, in one of the middle schools included in Phase I of the program, 90 percent of the students were receiving attention from programs for students in difficulty. In the years before the MOT Program was initiated, fully 70 percent of the students achieved below the levels set by the state and district for earned promotion and were retained in grade. The *average* student in that school took five years to complete the three years of the middle school. In one of the Phase I elementary schools, 90 percent of the students did reach the standards for earning promotion, but the median student's composite grade-level-equivalent was nearly a year behind the national average.

On the other hand, an "arts" magnet school provided an elaborate, vigorous, and highly successful program for a racially balanced population of students judged to have promise in one of the arts. The "arts" school was successful academically as well as in its thematic specialties. Unfortunately, its existence removed many of the most successful students from the other schools.

PREPROGRAM STAFF DEVELOPMENT PRACTICES

Prior to the inception of the MOT Program, nearly all the staff development elements were driven by requirements of some sort: for basic and specialized licenses, for curriculum changes, and for changes in the requirements of categorical programs. An unfortunate side-effect of the requirement-driven mode was that a large majority of teachers viewed staff development as something they must do to meet someone else's standard. Teachers in the district were (and are) required by the state and the district to earn a minimum of 10 credits either in university or district-sponsored courses each five years, and teachers could choose from a wide spectrum of offerings from the district's staff development office.

The curriculum unit offered workshops to support newly adopted materials, programs, and practices, and to disseminate regulations. Generally, the workshops were conducted either by representatives of the publishers of the textbooks or by district curriculum area coordinators, neither of which had used the materials in clssrooms. The workshops were largely for assistant principals and accompanied each new textbook adoption. After participating in the workshops, these assistant principals were to provide training to their school staffs. Where such training occurred, it was brief, expository, and unsystematic.

In addition, training was required as part of the system for evaluating new teachers. By the end of three years, teachers had to be qualified by an instrument that emphasized primarily the "direct teaching" approach interpreted from the work of Madeline Hunter. Principals and designated teachers were trained on the use of the beginning-teacher-evaluation model and, in conjunction with representatives of the state, observed the new teachers twice a year. The teachers being observed were expected to use some form of recitation teaching and illustrate their ability to execute the "Essential Elements of Instruction." Staff development was offered these new teachers based on their assessment profile.

Although nearly everyone in the district was concerned that student-achievement data from the testing program was almost flat from year to year, the staff development director was particularly concerned that the regular cycles of curriculum "adoption" and the large Title I programs were not improving instruction generally and that the offerings of the staff development unit were too weak to make much difference either. There was a good deal of evidence that many of the students were not being served well. Each year nearly one-sixth of the students in the district were suspended from school for one infraction or another, and the trend was upward. The number of students who failed to attain promotion was disturbing. Fewer than 10 percent of the students exited the Title I and special education programs in any year because of satisfactory performance.

The staff development director raised the question, "Could a staff development program, built around the study of instruction, result in sufficient change that student learning would increase?" From that question the project began to take shape.

PLANNING THE MOT PROGRAM: TRYING TO BUILD A COMMUNITY OF UNDERSTANDING

A six-month-long series of meetings were held with the district cabinet (superintendent, associate superintendent, assistant superintendents, and heads of departments), groups of principals, and teachers. The focus of the meetings was to approach the student-achievement problem through staff development focused on instruction.

A considerable amount of concept-building was necessary to build an understanding that would sustain a massive, concerted effort. Commonly used terms turned out to have radically different meanings for people. For example, during the initial discussions, some people thought of staff development as events, rather than as a process of study intended to influence what is taught and how it is taught. Some thought of instruction as the "province" of the curriculum department and expressed concern that there might be organizational problems if a major program sponsored by the staff development unit emphasized instruction.

During these initial discussions, the confusion was considerable. Officials responsible for curriculum, Title I, and special-education programs were not pleased to have the effectiveness of their programs called into question. The superintendent mediated the issues, arguing that doing things differently could be done with dignity— without "putting down" the present efforts, which were at least as good as the norm of the state and were well-administered compared to the programs of other districts. Nonetheless, the program planning might have bogged down in wrangling and inertia had not the state government made a general initiative in support of staff development. The state initiative precipitated the intensive planning that shaped the River City project and brought the district administrators together in a temporary alliance that facilitated forward movement.

THE STATE INITIATIVE IN STAFF DEVELOPMENT

During the spring the state legislature, with robust support from the governor, passed the Quality Basic Education Act (QBE). The act supported a substantial initiative in staff development, based on strong sentiment that few reforms would amount to much unless there was a strong staff development effort. The provisions of QBE included stipends for teachers to participate in summer programs related to instructional needs and made contributions to the administrative costs of staff development activities. Each of the state's 186 school districts received an allocation based on its number of teachers.

The staff development budgets of nearly all the state's districts had been very small. In River City, it was about $20 per teacher each year. The new act provided about $350 per employed teacher. A program that served 25 percent of the teachers in any district during a year would include resources of about $1,400 per teacher served.

The QBE guidelines did not prescribe the content of the programs to be mounted by the districts, and district personnel were given discretion to determine the content and the number of teachers to be served each year. For example, longer programs could serve 20 percent of the teachers, or shorter programs could serve a larger percentage. It was anticipated that the resources would be used primarily for summer programs because stipends could not be authorized except then, when teachers would be paid for service above their basic contracts. Important for supporting sustained school improvement was the expectation that QBE funding would continue for several years. Thus a district could decide to serve portions of its teachers and administrators each summer on a rotating basis.

The sudden influx of resources provided a great opportunity, but it also created problems for the districts to solve. Imagine the challenge for a district like River City, where the entire staff development program consisted of short courses driven by evaluation for license, requirements for recertification, and changes in textbooks with training provided by publishers' representatives. Some of the smaller districts had programs that contained no more than a half-dozen short workshops serving a few volunteer teachers or teachers seeking an initial license. Suddenly, these districts had to create staff development programs where virtually none had existed.

The resources provided by QBE enabled River City to proceed more rapidly and intensely than would otherwise have been the case. Eventually, about 40 percent of the district's allotment under the new act was used for the MOT Program. The remainder supported initiatives in special education and curriculum, permitted expanded responses to requests from schools, and helped with various smaller needs.

The need for rapid planning (only three months before the summer would begin) made the concept of the MOT Program, already partially planned, attractive to the district cabinet, partly because resources for it would not have to come from existing funds. The superintendent led the cabinet to a consensus on moving forward with the program, and detailed planning began. The project started to take shape.

MAKING THE DESIGN: CONTENT

The decision to focus on instruction that promised increased student learning had been explicit from the start. The question now became what kinds of student learning to emphasize and which instructional models to include. The district needed to reach for consultant help at this point, and what resulted was a partnership between the district and Booksend Laboratories that continued for several years and is reflected in the authorship of this article.

The district leaders and Booksend consultants worked together to survey available models of teaching that are backed up by a strong research base (Joyce and Weil 1986) and chose several that apply to a wide variety of curriculum areas. The chosen models also promised to make the instructional environment more active, to encourage higher order thinking skills, and to teach social skills and thereby increase the cooperative environment of the classroom and school.

Specifically, over the life of the program, the following models were used:

1. Various forms of basic cooperative-learning strategies

2. Inductive-thinking and concept-attainment models that teach students to develop, refine, and apply concepts

3. Synectics, a model to teach synthesis through the use of analogies

4. Mnemonics, specifically the link-word method for helping students to learn and retain new concepts and information

These models, used in conjunction with one another, address a variety of goals: social skills and values, development of self-esteem (by increasing ability to learn), increased ability to regulate one's own behavior and resolve conflicts, and increased ability to learn academic material by analyzing information, forming and refining concepts, synthesizing information, and using association devices to memorize and retain new material.

These models of teaching get their effects by teaching students an increased repertoire of learning skills. In the study of writing, for example, students skilled in using these models should have increased ability to work in cooperative groups and to analyze and produce writing, with confidence that their skills are increasing through simple application of the models.

The MOT Program was designed to help teachers *increase* their repertoires rather than replace their existing repertoires. The idea was to enhance and expand natural styles, rather than discarding them. A corollary was to help teachers focus on increasing the students' repertoires of models of learning. As it turned out, the above models of teaching represented real increases in repertoire for the teachers in River City. For nearly all teachers, *all* of these models provided them with approaches to teaching that significantly expanded the types of things they could do with their students.

The reader will recognize that the content of the program is one approach to what has been called "thinking skills," cooperative learning, and mastery learning, all undertaken simultaneously.

We attempted to design the training process to ensure implementation of the models. The schools in the program changed their operations to increase colleagueship and empower the faculties to make decisions about how to further improve the schools. The roles of administrative teams were changed to emphasize management of these school-improvement efforts. Support for these teams was extensive, helping them learn to lead their faculties to success.

MAKING THE DESIGN: CREATING A DECISION-MAKING MODALITY

Two decisions were then made that greatly affected the social and organizational character of the initiative. One was to concentrate the enterprise on schools as "wholes." The second was to accept schools on a voluntary basis, with faculties deciding if their school would apply.

The first decision came directly from the substantive objective of the initiative: to affect the environment of the school in such a way that students became more powerful learners, thus raising their rates of learning in the personal, social, and academic domains. If only a handful of teachers from any given school studied teaching models and added them to their effective repertoires, the learning environment of the school would be only modestly affected.

We reasoned that if we started with teams of volunteers the program would probably be history by the time we had reached a density in any one school critical enough to affect student learning. However, if all the teachers created cooperative classrooms that emphasized enriching the students' tools for learning, the effect on the environment should be sufficient to palpably affect student learning. *Thus, the initiative would touch only a few schools at a time, but would touch everyone in those schools.*

The second decision was an attempt to have participants make informed choices about participating, both in terms of the models of teaching they would be learning and in terms of the social process they would be joining. In other words, the process of having faculties "decide" to participate was designed to introduce these faculties to an informed, collegial process. Thus, after principals and teachers were provided with information about what the project would entail, they were to discuss whether they wanted to participate and arrive at a decision. To become a candidate for the initiative, a faculty had to demonstrate that at least 80 percent of their number had voted to participate and that *all the others understood they would have to participate also.*

In the five schools that became the leading candidates for the first year, all but one or two faculty members voted for the school to participate and those who didn't were chiefly concerned about interruptions to their planned summer schedules. Many other schools voted above the 80 percent level. By midspring, it was settled that two elementary schools and one middle school would begin.

(By the fifth year of the MOT Program in River City, 16 schools had participated fully, and there was a waiting list of schools that had sent teams to summer institutes. Many individual teachers and administrators had participated in workshops and short courses on specific models of teaching. The faculties of the schools that were "waiting in the wings" had many members who were familiar with the content and process of the program. By the end of that fifth year, about 1,200 of the 1,800 teachers in the district had been in courses as individuals or teams or were members of the "whole school" process.)

In reality, in that first year it was very difficult for faculties to make truly informed decisions because few could visualize so many new and unfamiliar components in operation. For example, the models of teaching were very different from the teachers' current repertoires, which was difficult for all but a few to imagine. (Most thought they came to the program with a "complete" repertoire.) Talks and discussions, however thorough, could not quite bridge the gap between past experience and what was to become current reality.

In subsequent years, other faculties could "see and feel" what had gone on in the first group of schools and make more informed decisions. The program elements we describe below had all been explained orally and in writing; understandably, the teachers could not envision them in practice. However, all the teachers had signed a detailed agreement that they understood each program element and were willing to participate in the process.

Collaborative decision-making was a new process to the faculties, and, despite the elaborate orientation and the provision of intricate decision-making procedures, collaboration in decision-making was unreal to many people. As they did it, they hardly believed it. Many faculties had never made a collective decision that bound all members, and many of their teachers were amazed that they could. Many could "mouth the words" of democratic decision-making and describe what they were doing, but the words were often tentative and did not sound natural.

MAKING THE DESIGN: PLANNING FOR FURTHER COLLEGIALITY

Although the models of teaching that were identified to initiate the project had been selected by the project coordinators, a major goal was to increase school-improvement inquiries initiated by the faculties themselves. The faculties had committed to two conditions designed to develop collegial problem-solving groups. One was to work together in study groups to support themselves in the implementation of new teaching repertoires. The second condition was to organize a building leadership team that would help the faculty study the health of the school and generate new initiatives for improvement, gradually taking over decision-making and program assessment. In the long run, it turned out that developing collective decision-making capability was far more difficult than the implementation of the models of teaching.

Like most school faculties, these teachers had worked largely in isolation, heeding the norms of "autonomy" that prevailed in the schools. They had rarely engaged in cooperative problem-solving and, of course, had no experience with innovations of the magnitude encompassed by the MOT Program. Most principals, although active, had been seen as managers and evaluators. Those principals were now to be full participants in the staff development sessions, were to participate in study groups, and were to organize their faculties to use the new content and to work together to develop new initiatives for improving their schools.

Even the first decision to participate violated the norms of autonomy so common in schools in that the decision of the majority (albeit a large majority) would obligate others. Fortunately for the beginning of the program, the first group of faculties had voted virtually unanimously in favor of participation so that no one had to feel coerced. For one or two persons in a faculty, ways to accommodate minority interests can always be found, and were. However, these faculties had committed themselves to practices very different from their normative ones, as we will see.

The collegial study of teaching was about to begin as was the process of learning to work together to make decisions.

MAKING THE DESIGN: SELECTING THE STAFF DEVELOPMENT MODEL

Related both to the study of teaching and the development of colleagueship was the model for designing workshops and the workplace generated by Showers and Joyce. The "peer coaching" model, as it is frequently called, enables 90 percent or more of teachers to reach, within two or three months, at least a routine, mechanical level of use of teaching practices previously unfamiliar to them. Teachers can begin to apply the new practices adequately almost immediately after training. Thus, the model, when implemented well, rarely loses in the wars of implementation of the training content.

The peer-coaching model is also compatible with the objective of increasing colleagueship in the workplace, for teachers work together in study groups to design lessons and units together, share their own development efforts, and study the effects on their students. In a real sense, it results in what has been called *collaborative action research* by those groups.

The peer-coaching model includes a distinction between *the design of workshops,* which need to impart a degree of knowledge and skill that will sustain practice in the school, and *the design of the workplace,* which includes the conditions in school that enable practitioners to work together until they have mastered the teaching skills that are the content of the training. The two designs need to be integrated, but the problems of organizing them are considerably different.

The Design of Training. The training design has three principal components: lectures, readings, and discussions created to develop theoretical understanding; demonstrations designed to provide behavioral descriptions of the procedures; and provisions for initial practice in the workshop setting.

Development of theoretical understanding. Understanding sustains best use, unless practice is to be rote and formulaic. Teachers need to know the conceptual base and thoroughly understand the kinds of effects to be expected if variations are appropriately used. They also need to know how to measure progress to determine if they are getting the desired effects. Without deep understanding, an innovation will be short-lived (see Fullan and Steigelbauer 1991 and Joyce and Showers 1995 for extensive treatments).

Knowledge of the expected magnitude of effects on student learning is extremely important, for it keeps the purpose of the training in the forefront and requires that trainers attempt to change the views that many practitioners have about achievement and its measures. Vague notions about "test scores" and "portfolio assessment," without clear views about what to expect and precisely how to measure outcomes, are of little use; consequently, devices for measuring effects on students may need to be included in the training.

Development of theoretical understanding also supports variations of the teaching strategy not included in initial training. Persons learning their first simple cooperative-learning technique should not deceive themselves that they have consumed the whole enchilada. They are just beginning their venture.

Behavioral representations: Modeling and demonstration. The fulcrum of training design is demonstration. Modeling anchors the theory in clarified behavior and provides the behavioral basis for skill development. Demonstrating with the teachers as "students" is useful, but it is no substitute for videotapes of children working. Especially needed are tapes that show how to organize students and provide them with instructions.

How much demonstration is needed? About 20 demonstrations are needed as a base for adequate skill development for a model of teaching of medium complexity. At least half of these demonstrations should be videotapes with students. We used about a dozen tapes to demonstrate even the simplest of techniques. Trainers need to keep in mind that participants, when they engage in their first trials in the classroom, tend to mimic closely what they have *seen* in training. Thus, demonstrations at an adult level, while very useful, should not be relied on exclusively.

Practice. Opportunities for practice need to be provided within the workshop setting. Teachers new to a procedure need practice especially in making the "opening moves" that start a teaching/learning episode. Skillful demonstrators bring the students into the process so smoothly that novices have trouble profiting from that aspect of the demonstration. Practice of the process during the workshop gives the trainer the opportunity to observe and to follow up these observations with further demonstrations that make critical skills manifest.

The combination of these three elements—providing for theoretical understanding, demonstration, and initial practice—enables nearly all teachers to develop a level of skill that will sustain practice in the classroom (Showers 1990), but the process of transfer to the workplace has just begun. *If nothing else is done, fewer than 10 percent of the teachers will be able to engage in enough practice to add the new procedures to their repertoire* (Joyce and Showers 1995). Thus, the design of the workplace and what will happen following the workshops is of paramount importance.

The Design of the Workplace. A mixture of understanding and skills is needed if transfer is to be accomplished. Participants have to navigate the distance between the training setting and their instructional setting. In the course of this process of transfer, their understanding will be deepened, their skills will mature, and, central to transfer, their understanding of when to use the procedure and how to increase the skills of the learner will develop.

Immediate and sustained practice. The first understanding is that practice in the classroom needs to be immediate and sustained. Delaying practice inevitably leads to a loss of understanding and skill. If there is any fear or skepticism about the use of the new procedure, delay gives anxiety time to develop and practice will not ensue. Thus, immediate practice is essential.

Second, about 20 to 30 trials with any new procedure are needed before control and comfort with it are achieved. Everyone needs to know this and to understand that the anxiety that often accompanies initial practice will diminish rapidly after the first half-dozen trials. Otherwise, participants will tend to avoid the anxiety by avoiding practice.

Sharing and peer coaching. Third, companionship and sharing (peer coaching) will greatly boost implementation. Thus, *prior to training*, teachers need to organize themselves into study groups who will share plans, discuss their experiences, and develop a sense of community as they struggle to bring about change in their behaviors. Observation is very helpful, for it enables members of study groups to pick up ideas from one another and to get a sense of their relative success. However, study-group members should be chary of offering advice to one another. They need to acknowledge that they are novices with the new procedure and may well offer poor advice without realizing it. We have watched more than one study group invent a dysfunctional variation on a model of teaching because the most forthcoming member of the group provided the wrong advice in a knowing manner.

Immediate and sustained practice, combined with companionship and boosted by observation, will ensure that nearly all persons will reach a routine but mechanical level of use with a new teaching procedure. Provided that practice occurs daily, this level should be reached in about six weeks and create readiness for the next workshop, which should occur about then.

Commitment to the above training and workplace conditions, by both participants and organizers, should be made *before* training commences. Organizers need to provide time for study groups to meet, facilitate classroom observations among study group members, and communicate any problems to the trainers conducting the workshops.

The consultant team was committed to be in residence for a two-week period for the initial summer training and six two-week periods for each of the first two years. The tasks were to visit teachers, study progress, and offer further workshops. Essentially, if this staff development design were implemented, we felt confident that virtually all teachers would reach a fair degree of mastery of their new models of teaching.

MAKING THE DESIGN: BUILDING IN A FORMATIVE-EVALUATION SYSTEM

The formative-evaluation system was designed to study implementation and progress toward the achievement of student-learning goals. It had three functions. One was to enable us to track implementation and adjust support accordingly. We would know how much each teacher was practicing, the levels of skill they manifested, and the problems they expressed. Thus workshops and consultation could be modulated on a real-world basis.

The second function of the formative-evaluation system was to orient the faculties and administrators toward data utilization. Using data, we reasoned, would help everyone in the program follow its progress and develop ownership of it. In addition, using data would help prepare the faculties for the self-directed action research that we hoped would develop. Thus, the formative component could be regarded as technical support or training for collegial action.

The third purpose of the formative system was to assess the effects of the project on teaching practice and the learning of students.

Thus, the system was structured to provide four kinds of information: (1) to track the implementation of the components of the program and guide their improvement; (2) to assess the effects on the learning opportunities of the students; (3) in certain areas, to attempt to determine whether the learning rates of the students accelerated; and (4) to study changes in the collegial interactions of the teachers.

The design included broad-scale surveys of the implementation of the components throughout the schools and intensive study of randomly selected classrooms. Data were obtained from a variety of sources:

1. Logs of the use of models of teaching were collected on a weekly basis from all teachers. These were used to determine amounts of practice and their self-estimates of their skill and the skill of their students in responding to the various models of teaching.

2. Minutes were collected each week from study groups. These minutes were used to document the content and types of interaction, including shared planning and the borrowing of ideas from one another.

3. Case studies were used. Six teachers were randomly selected from each of the three schools, observed and interviewed six times each year, and videotaped using their new repertoire. The data gathered from these teachers were analyzed to deter-

mine levels of use of the models, the skill they had achieved (including integrated use of the teaching strategies), their levels of comfort, problems encountered, and expressed needs.

4. Several student measures were used. Referrals and reports of subsequent disciplinary action were collected regularly; writing samples were collected from the students at intervals and used to determine changes in quality of writing; promotion records were collected annually; and standard tests of achievement were administered annually.

All these data were analyzed regularly and reported to the participating schools and teachers.

MAKING THE DESIGN: "THE CADRE"

The intention from the beginning of the program was to increase the capacity of the district to sustain and expand its school-improvement initiatives, thus reducing and then eliminating the need for external support. A primary means was the development of a community of teachers and administrators who could carry forth all phases of the initiative: introducing more schools to the processes outlined above, providing staff development on models of teaching, supporting study groups and building leadership teams, and giving help to other groups of schools.

The district design team decided to recruit the cadre from the pool of teachers who made outstanding progress with the models of teaching and who showed leadership in their schools in study groups and schoolwide organization. The first summer institutes included the 120 members of the faculties of the three schools, plus about 25 faculty members and administrators from other schools who volunteered to join the initial stages of the effort.

The implementation of the content by all these persons was studied as described above. In the spring, those wishing to be candidates for the cadre submitted videotapes of their use of each model in the classroom. These videotapes were evaluated by the Booksend team, who also visited those persons in their classrooms, watched them teach, and interviewed them.

An initial cadre of 20 persons was organized to receive training additional to the other teachers and administrators, training that included the processes of organizing faculties and study groups and the conduct of training.

MAKING THE DESIGN: THE PRINCIPALSHIP

The principalship was regarded as critical. As indicated earlier, the school administrators attended all training and were asked to practice the new teaching strategies. In addition to organizing and supporting study groups, they were members of study groups.

During the first summer, each of the principals, assistant principals, and a lead teacher from each participating school attended an *additional* summer institute of two weeks' duration offered to teams from across the country to study models of teaching, processes of staff development, and the school-improvement process. During that summer, these administrators and teacher leaders studied models of teaching and school improvement for a month and prepared detailed plans for their conduct of the project.

During the school year, these same administrators and teachers were involved in regular meetings to discuss the initiative, assess progress, and receive consultation. In addition, regular private meetings were held by the Booksend team with each principal/assistant-principal team to discuss progress and try to develop solutions to problems. About 12 such meetings were held with each team during the first year.

COMMUNICATING AND GETTING GOING

All the above information about the training design was communicated in sets of meetings to the district office personnel, all the district principals, and groups of teachers throughout the district, as well as the personnel directly involved in the operation of the program. Dates were set and the program began.

THE RIVER CITY MOT PROGRAM: YEAR 1

Much of this narrative will report the events of the first year and try to interpret the information in relation to the problems of changing the culture of education. We start this narrative with a description of what happened in the middle school.

THE MIDDLE SCHOOL

We really didn't know, as the project began, just how desperate things were at the middle school. Imagine a school that loses a third of its faculty each year to transfer, requested by the teachers, and does not have a full staff until the first day of the school year because hardly anybody wants to work there. Imagine 15 newly assigned teachers, fearful of the children, hoping to get through the year and transfer out. Among them are a few long-term teachers, some *very* committed to the children, trying to orient the newcomers to the place and help them find materials. The children arrive: poor, black, upset. The front door appears to revolve as the students are "sent to the office" and suspended. (Of 550 kids, half were suspended the year before the project began.)

Dispirited is too mild a word to describe the children. For many of the eighth graders, this is their fifth year in the school. Only about one-third of the students manage to pass the tests that earn promotion at the end of a year. The year before the project began, only 4 of the 154 seventh-grade students earned promotion. Thus, the seventh grade as our year 1 begins is filled with students who failed the previous year.

The picture on standard tests revealed that the average child in the school has been progressing about 60 percent as rapidly as the average child in the nation. Our seventh graders here, academically speaking, were fourth graders, and many could not read effectively. Yet, the textbook-driven curriculum depended on reading, and promotion depended on passing the tests the publishers supply with the textbooks. Many of these middle-school students were third graders in terms of achievement. And, in standard test terms, *there were no high achievers.* No child had been able to overcome the environment and score as high as the 60th percentile on any standard test.

June of 1987 comes and the faculty of the middle school file into the high school along with the faculties of the two elementary schools, a collection of interested parties from a variety of other schools, and a number of central-office personnel. The project begins with a summer institute introducing the faculties to three models of teaching.

The first week of this two-week summer institute is in June; the second week is in August. The theory-demonstration-practice cycle is followed as the new models are introduced. The faculties are organized into teams who are to meet weekly between the institutes. They are to build lessons they will use when school opens in the fall and share these with each other.

How does our middle school faculty react to all this? First, with disbelief. The thing is really happening! We discover that most of the staff of all three schools had not thought the project would really happen as designed when they agreed to participate in it! Now, it turns out that they are really expected to use these models of teaching and that data will be collected to determine the nature of their planning and practice. Second, they react with shock and surprise to the idea that anyone really thinks that complex models of learning are appropriate for the children they teach. Quite simply, they think we are crazy. They are not alone. A fair number of the elementary school faculties agree with them, though the proportion in agreement is smaller.

We asked them why. They are not reticent about telling us. In their opinion, the students are not capable of constructing knowledge. And, these students will "go out of control" in cooperative settings.

Note that we had a number of choices as we perceived this reaction. Nearly all the middle-school teachers were rejecting the content. Not all, of course. The assistant principal and several teachers were very enthusiastic and getting ready to dig in and make the project work. Should we let the others withdraw? Should we draw back and plan more training before they tried to use the models? Or should we give the "commitment follows competence" theory a real test and trust the "training model."

WE PRESSED ON

We made our own interpretations of what they said. From our perspective, part of their reaction derived from their stated view of the kids: "The kids are genetically incapable of complex learning." "Their home backgrounds compound the problem of their native lack of ability."

Some of the teacher's reactions pertained to the efficacy of education: "The school is powerless in the face of the quality of the children and the homes."

Part of the reaction dealt with the district and us:"You will never follow up. Maybe this stuff could work, but we need a lot more help than you will be willing to give us. When we try these things and run into trouble, you won't be there."

We responded directly. First, the kids can learn and teachers can make it happen. Second, the school is not powerless. Third, we would be there. We were no more subtle than they were. And, somehow, they did create lessons and got ready for the fall, still skeptical of the content and of us and of the commitment by the district. But, they were ready to give it a try. The elementary school teachers were, as a group, less skeptical than the middle school teachers, but nearly all were nervous that they might be in a situation where they were being asked to challenge the students beyond their ability to respond.

SCHOOL BEGINS

The building leadership teams were ready and put the plan for practice and study groups into action. The study groups met, lessons were designed around the models and used, logs were kept of practice, and the principals were supportive and firm. The consultants showed up, to nearly everyone's surprise, and visited every teacher in every classroom, met with study groups and, still more surprising, taught lessons themselves—which they videotaped and showed to the teachers. In the middle school, the assistant principal and a counselor created and taught lessons daily and sometimes several times a day. The project director visited each school weekly for the better part of a day, was in and out of classrooms, talked with the teachers and children, and encouraged the administrators.

The teachers practiced their models, met in their groups, and suffered their anxiety, still skeptical. They practiced their cooperative, inductive, concept-attainment, and mnemonics models regularly. When the administration of the middle school and the consultants found that many of the teachers were tentative about using cooperative groups, even dyads, they persuaded the faculty to have "cooperative learning days" where every student would experience some form of cooperative activity every period throughout the day. The assistant principal was able to report to the faculty that referrals for disciplinary action dramatically dropped on those days!

Overt expressions of skepticism continued, but the teachers became aware that the kids were becoming easier to manage and, most important, that they could respond to the models. The kids began doing their homework. The teachers reported less "back talk" from the children.

As the time for "end of unit" tests came and went, nearly all the teachers reported that the results were far better than they had ever experienced before.

THE TEACHING OF WRITING

In the middle school, the consultants and assistant principal discovered that, in the past, very little writing had been elicited from the children because the faculty felt that they couldn't write. Believing that they never would learn to write without practice, we initiated a drive to ensure that each student was asked to write at least two or three times a week. An English teacher new to the middle school took up the challenge powerfully and made sure that all the eighth-grade students wrote regularly. By midyear it was apparent to everyone that eighth-grade writing was beginning to improve, and by the end of the year it had improved substantially. Her example influenced many of the other teachers.

The situation was similar in the elementary schools, but teachers gradually realized the importance of practice and more and more teaching/learning episodes included writing.

Throughout the year, teachers gradually attained mastery over their new teaching strategies and used them more and more appropriately. But before we discuss transfer and the effects on student learning, we need to examine the state of colleagueship.

THE STUDY GROUPS

As we mentioned earlier, the collegial arrangements represented quite a departure from traditional practice in the schools, as cooperative teacher work clashed structurally with the customs attendant to autonomous teaching. Each school's faculty organized itself into study groups of four to six persons, and the administrators arranged for them to meet weekly.

Although few teachers saw the opportunity for their empowerment through colleagueship that we envisioned, they generally welcomed the opportunity to get together. The need for adult interaction appeared to be very much present. Study groups offered an opportunity to socialize that had been absent. However, many teachers were somewhat nervous about getting together at first for reasons we were not prepared for.

One reason given was anxiety about whether cooperative teacher work was legitimate. (That concern appears to have stemmed from the fact that the evaluation of teachers was traditionally performed on an individual basis; some teachers inferred that cooperative work would collide with the evaluation system. The concern appears to be similar to the frequently voiced problem of how to "grade" students who work in cooperative groups and produce collective products.) Some teachers really worried that the principals may have been "violating a rule" by providing cooperative planning time during the day.

A second concern was that the cooperative planning of lessons was almost "cheating" on the job. It's as if the norms of autonomous practice were so ingrained that cooperative teaching violated the provisions of their contract.

A third concern was that cooperative planning violates professional integrity if it is a regular part of work, unlike, say, a couple of teachers getting together occasionally on a voluntary basis. Nonetheless, the groups met and the principals assured them that it was okay to do so.

However, as we visited the study groups it appeared that, unless a strong, natural, conceptual leader emerged quickly and structured the planning activities, the groups were confused about what to do. Most of the folks were completely inexperienced in cooperative planning and how to go about it. The consultants were drawn on for a great deal of advice, some of it minute, about what to plan together and how to go about it, what to share and how, and how to observe one another without being offensive.

As the study groups learned to engage in the originally planned tasks, to construct and try lessons together, and to share and discuss their individual projects, some fresh resistance to the teaching strategies developed. The resistance was not by any means universal, but it was there, and its causes appeared to be several. Teachers accustomed to following instructional materials closely and "letting the textbook do the planning" sometimes found that thinking through lessons was onerous work. Some of them appeared afraid of being exposed as conceptually inadequate. A few felt that asking for help was a sign of weakness. A few wondered if colleagues were a legitimate source of help. They were not sure their colleagues knew enough.

Some novice teachers and others new to the system worried that the use of these models of teaching might conflict with the beginning-teacher-observation system. Principals and assistant principals were a great help in allaying this fear, particularly because they were in evaluative roles, but the anxiety continued for some time. Imagine the dilemma of a young teacher afraid that an evaluator will catch him or her teaching through inductive thinking or cooperative learning or, ye gods, both! Given these concerns, the study of implementation and student learning was extremely important as we tried to assess progress and modulate the support accordingly.

THE STUDY OF IMPLEMENTATION: DESIGN

The chief implementation questions were derived from the two-fold nature of the program: appropriate use of alternative models of teaching (substantive content of training) and implementation of change in the workplace, specifically opportunity and ability to work with colleagues on the appropriate implementation of an innovation aimed at increased student learning. These specific questions were explored:

1. Did the faculties implement the content of the training? (That is, what levels of use and what degrees of transfer of training were achieved with the models of teaching in which teachers were trained?)

2. What factors affected variation in faculties' use of the models of teaching? (That is, did cohesiveness of faculties and peer-coaching study teams, individual growth states, grade level, age, and experience affect implementation?)

3. Did changes in the workplace occur as a result of whole-faculty participation in the project, specifically the development of the ability of the faculty and administration to set specific goals for school improvement?

SAMPLE

One hundred and sixteen teachers and administrators—the faculties from the first three schools—were involved in this first study of implementation. Although data were collected on all of them, the bulk of this report deals with case studies of a subset of 18 teachers— 6 from each of the 3 target schools—who were selected on a stratified random basis. The case-study sample for each of the two elementary schools included one teacher from each grade level (K-5) and, for the middle school, two teachers from each of grades 6, 7, and 8. A second-grade teacher was dropped from the sample because of an extended illness that required her early retirement.

The remaining 17 teachers included 7 new or probationary teachers, 5 teachers who had taught from 5 to 10 years, 3 who had taught from 11 to 20 years, and 2 who had more than 20 years' experience. Apparently the percentage of new teachers in our random sample (35 percent) was not characteristic of the district as a whole but was in fact typical of these particular schools; teachers with greater seniority in the system have traditionally transferred out of these low-socio-economic-status (SES) schools. Sixteen of the 17 teachers were female, and the entire sample participated in the two-week summer training session prior to the first year of the project.

PROCEDURES USED IN THE IMPLEMENTATION STUDY

Six times during the 1987-88 academic year, teachers in the sample were observed in their classrooms and informally interviewed regarding their use of models.

Teachers were asked to maintain monthly logs detailing their use of the teaching models on which they had received training during the summer of 1987. All teachers in the sample complied with this request, though there were missing data for some for an occasional month.

Arrangements were made to videotape teachers in the sample near the end of the first project year to determine skill levels with various models of teaching. Videotapes were completed for 14 of these 17 teachers.

Formal interviews regarding teacher use and attitudes toward the teaching strategies that were the object of this implementation effort were completed with all sample teachers in April 1988 and again in January 1989.

Sixteen of the sample teachers attended a second two-week training session during the summer of 1988 and were studied during their second year of implementation. The procedures for examining implementation were identical to those used in the first year of the project.

THE STUDY OF PRACTICE AND LEVELS OF TRANSFER

The study of practice was combined with the study of levels of transfer in terms of skill attained with the models.

Practice. Amount of practice was simply a tabulation of the number of trials per month reported by the teachers in their logs. These data are reasonably accurate representations of practice, but they are not perfect. Some teachers recorded every lesson while others recorded only examples of different types of lessons. The six informal interviews recorded during the year as well as the formal interviews helped validate the information recorded on logs and make the picture of practice as correct as possible.

Levels of Transfer. "Levels of Transfer" is a continuum with a score of 1 (low) to 5 (high).

Level 1 represents *imitative use*, that is, a replication of lessons demonstrated in training settings. The types of lessons selected for imitation often represent only the most simple and concrete examples of a class of demonstrations. For example, if a cooperative numbered-heads activity were demonstrated with a list of spelling words during training, and teachers were subsequently observed to use numbered heads only with their spelling lists, their level of transfer would be judged to be imitative, though appropriate. Likewise, the fact that various forms of more complex cooperative activity had been demonstrated during training but were absent from early practice was characterized as Level 1.

Level 2 indicates *mechanical use* (or horizontal transfer) in that the same teacher who was using numbered-heads activities only for spelling begins to use numbered heads for drills in reading vocabulary, addition and multiplication facts, and so forth. Practice increases at this level, but there is little variation in types of implementation. More complex examples of the models of teaching learned during training continue to be missing from teacher practice.

Level 3 is a *routine* level of transfer in that certain activities, types of lessons, and objectives become identified with specific models of teaching. For example, as students learn the states and capitals of the United States, geographic features of regions of the country, and major land forms and oceans of the world, teachers routinely select mnemonic strategies to accomplish their objectives. Use of the strategies is frequent at this stage, but alternative strategies are not considered at this point, nor are curriculum objectives thought of in other than a lower order, concrete fashion.

Level 4 transfer is called *integrated use* and generally occurs for different models at different rates. For example, a teacher who has frequently used mnemonic strategies for learning concrete bits of information in multiple subjects begins to understand that sequences of events in history, major points in a philosophy, and policy issues faced by presidents and governors are also areas for application of mnemonic strategies. The proportion of imitative to innovative, subject-specific use has become quite small.

Finally, Level 5 transfer is designated as *executive control* of the content of training. Executive control is characterized by complete understanding of the theories underlying the various models learned, a comfortable level of appropriate use for varieties of models of teaching, and consequently the ability to select specific models and combinations of models for objectives within a unit as well as across subject areas.

Integrated curriculum objectives as well as higher order objectives are frequently observable at this fifth level. Thus, a teacher introducing a piece of literature to fifth-grade students might begin with objectives relating to understanding of the relationships that evolve between certain characters in the book. The teacher may also employ inductive-thinking, concept-attainment, mnemonic, and cooperative strategies to teach the necessary vocabulary and word-attack skills to enable the students to read the story with comfort. The major emphases, however, will be on analysis of the relationships between characters through categorization and interpretation of key passages from the piece and writing with analogies to examine the changing nature of evolving relationships.

Lesson plans, interviews, logs, and protocols from observations were analyzed to determine the levels of transfer achieved by the teachers. For each teacher, all lessons reported on logs and six systematic observations during each year of the project provided data for determining transfer level. Interview data supplemented lesson plans and observations with self-reports on teachers' use of the models of teaching in their classrooms. Each lesson analyzed was assigned a score of 1 (imitative use) to 5 (executive control), and means were computed for each teacher.

PERSONAL CHARACTERISTICS: STATES OF GROWTH

To examine factors that were hypothesized to affect variation in teachers' use of the models of teaching, *states of growth* (an orientation to the external environment with respect to both the formal and informal opportunities for professional development) were calculated for each teacher. State-of-growth data were derived from interviews and observations of study teams. Data on teachers' grade level, age, and experience were available from employment records housed both at the school and at the central office.

McKibbin and Joyce (1980) derived the states-of-growth measure in their study of staff development in California. Through a structured-interview process, they examined teachers' and administrators' responses to opportunities for professional development through the formal staff development system offered by universities, counties, state-sponsored agencies, and districts; the informal opportunities provided by peers; and the participation in nonprofessional, personal-growth opportunities available in the general environment (books, film, theater, and so forth).

In the study reported by McKibbin and Joyce, teachers who participated fully in both formal and informal professional-development activities also tended to have well-developed interests in the personal domain; that is, teachers who were actively reaching out for growth opportunities in their professional lives were generally engaged in growth. Furthermore, teachers characterized by high growth states were more likely to implement innovations for which they received training and to achieve transfer of those innovations into their active teaching repertoires.

In a study by Evans and Hopkins (1988), in which both growth states of individual teachers and climate ratings of the schools in which they taught were examined for their influence on teacher implementation of training, growth states was found to be a more powerful predictor of implementation than was school climate (though the latter was not without effect).

The growth-states hierarchy is described in full in several sources (Joyce, Bush, and McKibbin 1982; McKibbin and Joyce 1980; Joyce and Showers 1995), but briefly, the categories are as follows:

Gourmet Omnivores are individuals who not only reach out for opportunities in their environments but who generate or initiate those opportunities for themselves and others. These individuals are active participants in many growth opportunities but are discriminating about their choice of activities. They are knowledgeable about the range of options available to them. According to Joyce and Showers, gourmet omnivores are "mature high-activity people who have learned to canvass the environment and exploit it successfully" (1988, p. 134).

Active Consumers are similar to gourmet omnivores in that they continually scan their environments for growth opportunities and take advantage of those opportunities in both the professional and personal domains. They differ from gourmet omnivores in that they are less initiating and less likely to create opportunities and options where none exist.

Passive Consumers comprised about 70 percent of the initial sample in the California Staff Development Study (Joyce, Bush, and McKibbin 1982). They are characterized as amiable, conforming, and highly dependent on their immediate social context. They attended required staff development programs but seldom did anything with the content, and the activities engaged in outside the work setting depended very much on whether their families and friends initiated such activities.

Reticents actually "expend energy pushing away opportunities for growth. . . . they have developed an orientation of reluctance to interact positively with their cultural environment" (Joyce and Showers 1988, p. 136). Consequently, reticents resist opportunities for growth and often perceive efforts by peers or administrators to effect change as forms of conspiracy designed to leave them less powerful and efficacious.

EXTENT OF IMPLEMENTATION

What was the state of implementation and what factors contributed to it?

PRACTICE

Knowing that skill development requires a certain amount of practice before fluid and appropriate use is possible, we encouraged teachers at the three project schools to practice their newly learned models of teaching frequently, especially at the beginning of the school year immediately following training. In earlier studies, teachers who had postponed practice found it difficult or impossible to use the content of training. We urged teachers to implement the simpler forms of cooperative learning immediately and pervasively during the first month of school in order to teach students how to work in cooperative groups and to ease the implementation of other models of teaching.

Teachers were so successful in this effort that by the end of the first month most of the elementary teachers were reporting a minimum of two cooperative sessions per day and the middle school teachers at least four per week. In fact, one elementary teacher reported 80 trials with cooperative learning during the four weeks of September! Teachers found it much more difficult to implement the concept-attainment, mnemonic, and inductive-thinking strategies.

In table 2.1, reports of practice with cooperative learning are eliminated from the totals, and teachers who reported at least daily use of cooperative-learning strategies are indicated with a double asterisk.

Analysis of teacher logs for the 1987-88 academic year shows that, for our random sample of teachers, the new models of teaching were practiced an average of 14.48 times per month (for School A, 16.8; for School B, 11.1; and for School C, 14.98). During the second year, the average monthly use of models was 22.73 (for School A, 14.8; for School B, 24.4; and for School C, 29.0).

The question of greater concern to us, however, was the level of transfer of training to teachers' active repertoires: How appropriately were the new strategies being used? If teachers did not develop at least a routine level of transfer during the first year, would they ultimately develop integrated use and executive control with these models of teaching?

Table 2.2 summarizes the levels of transfer achieved by our sample during the project, except for cooperative learning (which was used frequently by all the teachers).

For year 1, the mean transfer-of-training score for our sample was 3.3 (routine use). Of the 17 teachers, 3 were still largely operating at the imitative stage (level 1); 3 had reached a mechanical level (level 2); and the remaining 11 had developed routine or integrative-use levels of transfer. Thus, while 15 of the 17 teachers were practicing frequently enough to develop skill in the new models of teaching, only 11 (65 percent) were using the strategies appropriately enough during the first project year to predict that their students would derive the intellectual, social, and personal benefits promised by research underlying the models.

In the second year of the project, the mean was also 3.3. The teachers in two of the three schools had increased both their practice

T A B L E   2.1

AVERAGE MONTHLY PRACTICE BY TEACHER WITH THREE MODELS OF TEACHING FOR TWO YEARS*

School	Teacher	Average Monthly Practice* 1987-88	1988-89
A	A**	19.6	20
	B**	13.0	20
	C	11.0	8
	D**	23.0	—
	E	15.6	14
	F	18.6	12
B	A**	18.0	40
	B**	20.0	38
	C**	10.1	20
	D	3.6	10
	E	3.7	14
C	A**	14.3	36
	B**	12.0	28
	C**	12.8	24
	D**	13.6	28
	E	17.2	—
	F**	20.0	29
		X = 14.5	X = 22.73
		S.D. = 5.4	S.D. = 10.3

*Excluding cooperative-learning lessons.

**Teachers who used cooperative learning one or more times per day.

and levels of transfer with models of teaching, while the third school (School A) actually suffered losses in both areas. Possible school-level causes for both gains and losses will be discussed later.

Frequency of practice with the models was correlated with level of transfer at r = .62 (Spearman Rank Correlation Coefficient) during year 1 of the project and at r = .75 during the second year. *Clearly, as is apparent in tables 1 and 2, no one reached high levels of transfer without frequent and consistent practice.* However, several teachers continued practice of the new strategies without apparently developing greater understanding of their use. They continued to imitate

T A B L E   2.2

TRANSFER OF TRAINING OF THREE MODELS OF TEACHING FOR TWO YEARS

School	Teacher	Transfer of Training 1987-88	1988-89
A	A	3.1	3.0
	B	4.0	4.5
	C	1.8	1.0
	D	4.7	—
	E	3.1	2.5
	F	3.8	3.0
B	A	4.3	4.5
	B	4.6	5.0
	C	3.5	3.5
	D	2.0	1.5
	E	1.9	2.5
C	A	3.6	3.5
	B	4.4	4.0
	C	2.5	3.0
	D	2.0	2.0
	E	1.9	—
	F	4.9	5.0
Mean		3.3	3.3

Levels of Transfer: 1 = imitative use; 2 = mechanical use; 3 = routine use; 4 = integrated use; 5 = executive use.

lessons they had observed with trainers or peers and found it difficult to depart from their teacher's manuals to experiment with alternative strategies for achieving similar instructional objectives.

FACTORS AFFECTING VARIATION IN USE AND TRANSFER

This project involved the entire faculties of three schools in the training and implementation of innovations for school improvement. We hypothesized that individual characteristics (states of growth, years of teaching experience), small-group characteristics (functioning of study groups), and school variables (principal leadership, faculty cohesion) might all affect teachers' rates of implementation. Here's what we learned.

Individual Factors. Growth-states scores were computed for all teachers in our sample near the end of the first project year (see table 2.3).

The mean growth state for our sample was 3.1 (S.D. = .96, range 1-5), with the mean for School A at 2.67, School B at 3.0, and School C at 3.5. As reported by both McKibbin and Joyce (1983) and Evans and Hopkins (1988), states of growth has proved to be a powerful predictor of implementation of innovations, both in projects involving whole schools as well as those involving only volunteers. *In this project, in which entire faculties participated if 80 percent or greater of their teachers requested the program, states of growth correlated .87 with transfer levels during year 1 and .88 during year 2 (Spearman Rank Correlation Coefficients).*

A common belief among both professional educators and the general public is that young teachers (those just entering the profession) are more open to innovation than older, more experienced teachers who have presumably become tired and set in their ways. The Joyce, McKibbin, and Bush (1982) study found no relationship between years of teaching experience and the willingness and ability to engage in professional growth. The good news from their study was that mature, experienced teachers are often at the height of their professional powers, while the bad news was that some young teachers just entering the profession are actively pushing away growth opportunities—they have quit learning at age 22.

We examined the relationship between years of teaching experience and transfer of training for our sample and found an r of .13 for the first year of the project and .10 for the second year. (A high positive correlation would have favored mature teachers while a high

T A B L E   2.3

TEACHER GROWTH STATES AND TRANSFER OF TRAINING OF THREE MODELS OF TEACHING

State of Growth	Transfer of Training		Mean Transfer Score
	1987-88	1988-89	
1	1.8	1.0	1.4
2	1.9	2.5	
2	2.0	1.5	2.2
2	3.1	2.5	
3	3.1	3.0	
3	4.0	4.5	
3	3.8	3.0	
3	3.5	3.5	2.8
3	3.6	3.5	
3	2.5	3.0	
3	2.0	2.0	
4	4.7	—	
4	4.4	4.0	4.5
4	4.3	4.5	
4	4.6	5.0	
5	4.9	5.0	4.95

Growth States: 1 = Reticent (satisfaction of basic needs); 2 = Withdrawn (psychological safety); 3 = Passive Consumer (concerns for belonging and security); 4 = Active Consumer (achievement orientation); 5 = Gourmet Omnivore (self-actualizing).

negative correlation would have favored beginning teachers.) Thus, for our sample, years of teaching experience were not associated with ability to transfer training into regular classroom practice.

Peer Group Influences. All teachers in the three project schools were members of peer-coaching study teams that were organized during the initial two-week workshop to facilitate the implementation of models of teaching. Study teams met weekly at the school sites on schedules worked out by the members of the teams in conjunction with their administrators.

The charge to study teams was threefold and emphasized only activities that were believed to increase practice with and implementation of the newly learned teaching strategies: teachers were to share lessons and materials already used in case others could use the plans/materials and thus cut down on preparation time; they were to observe each other trying the new strategies to learn from each other and study student responses to the strategies; and they were to plan future applications of the strategies within their curriculum areas in an attempt to integrate models' use with existing repertoires and instructional objectives.

Study-group functioning was conceived on a continuum from the merely pro forma, in which teachers meet as scheduled, verbally share experiences of lessons they have attempted with new models of teaching, and observe each other as scheduled; to enthusiastic participation, in which teachers share lessons they have taught, exchange materials they have developed, and observe each other easily and frequently to learn from each other; to fully collegial groups, in which teachers move beyond enthusiastic participation to the setting of common goals and the development of lessons and units that all or part of the group will use in the future.

In the first year, none of our sample teachers belonged to a fully collegial study group, though some of the groups occasionally worked in a fully collegial fashion for several weeks at a time. Twelve of our 17 sample teachers, however, belonged to "enthusiastic" groups whose members shared past lessons and materials freely and increasingly observed each other at unscheduled times because they enjoyed seeing each other try out lessons. The remaining five teachers belonged to pro forma groups and were passive members of those groups, neither complaining about the static nature of their meetings nor initiating more dynamic activities.

One is tempted to view the way the study groups functioned as a glass half empty, given the shortfall between what was possible and what occurred. However, we viewed the glass as half full. Consider that, prior to the project, teachers in the project schools never saw each other work, rarely met to discuss matters of curriculum and instruction (unless one counts monthly faculty meetings), and, with three exceptions, shared no lesson planning or materials development even though five or six teachers in a school might be teaching the same grade level or subject and using exactly the same texts. The implementation of study teams in the project schools did, in fact, greatly reduce the isolation in which most teachers formerly worked. Furthermore, the level of study-team functioning correlated .61 with transfer of training during the first year of the project.

Study-team functioning during the second year was much more mixed. The organization and facilitation of study teams requires active administrative support, not only for scheduling but for maintaining focus and purpose. One of the schools (School A) lost a very active administrator and gained a new (first-time) administrator. The same school, half-way though the second year, was "raided" by an administrator who was assembling faculty for a new school. Thus the School A teachers knew that nine of their number had been selected for the new school and would be leaving at the end of the year. This combination of factors was reflected in less practice for School A, declining rates of transfer, and lower study-team functioning during year 2 of the project. In the other two schools, two of the teams achieved fully collegial status; two alternated between enthusiastic and fully collegial functioning; four groups functioned at an enthusiastic level; and two functioned at a pro forma level.

Study-team functioning was influenced by the states of growth of individual members. Teams were generally comprised of four to six teachers. The four most successful study teams all had leadership from active consumers or gourmet omnivores. The presence of an active, growth-oriented individual, however, was not sufficient to ensure fully collegial functioning if one or more members were reticent or withdrawn. Study teams comprised of passive consumers were often enthusiastic but needed occasional help with structure. For example, they would approach the project consultants and ask for ideas or development projects to work on. They would then work enjoyably on a new idea, unit, or materials-development scheme until it was finished, then request more input.

The formation of study teams may be of interest to some readers. Faculty members formed their own groups. At first, these were generally grade-level teams. Gradually, over several years, more groups became more divergent, with members seeking greater variety of membership as they sought to expand their knowledge and colleagueship. If a self-selected group of reticents formed, an administrator joined this group to support implementation.

On balance, we believe the study teams functioned to boost implementation of innovations in our project schools, to increase teacher interaction about curriculum and instruction, and to reduce the norms of privacy and isolation. We do not believe, however, that the organization and functioning of study teams alone can change the climate of a school and create fully collegial interactions where few or none existed before, at least not in two years. Perhaps given the long tradition of school cultures in which teachers have had so little opportunity to work in collegial fashions and make collective decisions, time will be required to develop truly collegial patterns of work. Whether this means more years or more intensive time together is not clear to us at this point. We are convinced, however, that collegiality will develop only in conjunction with meaningful and challenging reasons for collaborative work, such as efforts to improve curriculum and instruction for increased student learning.

School-Level Factors. We have already mentioned the role of administrative leadership in the organization and functioning of study teams. Principals and assistant principals performed several other roles as well. First, they were instrumental in their school's participation in the project, since schools were not considered for inclusion unless 80 percent or more of the staff members were interested and principals wrote letters of application. Second, principals provided varying amounts of pressure and support with respect to practice of the new strategies.

During the first year, administrators in Schools A and B not only regularly observed (separate from "formal evaluation" observations) and encouraged teachers as they tried the new strategies but also borrowed classes and practiced the new strategies themselves. Administrators in Schools A and B met with study groups, and administrators in School C designated two lead teachers to meet with study groups and assist them during the first few months of the project. At Schools A and B, administrators generated schoolwide implementation projects for specific models of teaching during the first year, and during the second year, this activity was continued and increased in Schools B and C.

Since project consultants met regularly with administrators and encouraged their active leadership and participation, we cannot predict what the absence of administrative support would have meant to the project. However, the lessening of administrative support at School A during the second year and the concomitant losses there suggest that the support of administrators was crucial to project success.

Changes in the Workplace. Structural changes in the ways teachers worked with each other have already been discussed in the section on study teams. Possible increases (or decreases) in general cohesion and problem-solving ability can best be illustrated by what happened at the end of the project. Schools B and C retained their study-group formats, selected curriculum areas to focus on (schoolwide) and set goals for student achievement in those areas, secured additional training from consultants in their respective curriculum areas, and began working on the integration of models of teaching with new training in content and materials.

School A, at the close of the project, was struggling to retain its study-group format and incorporate 11 new staff members who had not had training in models of teaching. The principal was talking of retiring, and the new assistant principal was gamely trying to coordinate some sort of school-improvement focus for the year but had no consensus from the staff two months into the school year.

Implementation of the content of training was achieved at all three sites, though individual differences occurred. Given the history of implementation of curricular and instructional innovations (Fullan and Pomfret 1977; Joyce and Showers 1983, 1988), the implementation of models of teaching by three school faculties for whom the models represented additions to repertoire was a considerable achievement. Sufficient training was provided so that all teachers were able to practice their newly acquired skills, and teachers and administrators were able to restructure the workplace to the extent that teachers could regularly work together on implementation questions.

At the end of the first project year, 88 percent of the teachers were using the new strategies regularly and skillfully enough (a mechanical level of transfer or higher) that students had developed the requisite skills for learning within the models' frameworks. Sixty-seven percent of the teachers had achieved a routine or better level of transfer and thus had very good prospects for integrating the new models into their regular teaching repertoires.

It is difficult to determine how enduring even large structural and attitudinal changes will be at specific school sites. Clearly, stability of staff and administration are important, as are shared experiences in decision-making and training. It is probable that norms of continual renewal for individuals and faculties must extend beyond specific schools to entire districts and the profession at large before even large-scale change efforts can have long-range prospects for durability.

STANCE OF THE CENTRAL OFFICE

Although the cadre and many of the principals became more effective and built themselves a "learning community," many of the central-office personnel stood aloof from the project or even attacked it on various grounds. Some of these persons had administered "at risk" and other programs that had failed to improve student learning. Others appeared to realize that the program used teaching strategies, training designs, and collaborative decision-making modalities that lay outside their repertoire. Instead of participating in the MOT initiative, they persisted in generating curricular and organizational changes that were within their current range of skills.

EFFECTS ON STUDENTS

As the teachers learned to use models of teaching, the learning rates of the students began to improve.

THE MIDDLE SCHOOL

By the end of the first year, 70 percent of the students in the middle school achieved the standards required for promotion, and 95 percent earned promotion at the end of the second year. Judging from the results of standardized tests administered at the end of the second year, the average students in the school were achieving at a normal rate, that is, gaining 10 months of learning for 10 months of effort when compared to the United States population as a whole.

Time lost in disciplinary action decreased dramatically, to about one-fifth of the amount lost before the program began. Probably, helping the students learn a variety of learning strategies that enabled them to educate themselves more successfully reduced the incidences of discipline, for students who experience success in the classroom have less reason (and less time) to express their dissatisfaction with school in socially inappropriate ways.

At the end of the second year the social-studies test from the Iowa Tests of Basic Skills Battery was administered to all the middle school students (state and local regulations permitted the use of only the social-studies test). Thirteen eighth-grade students (8 percent of the class) scored 10.0 or greater in grade-level-equivalent terms (over the 84th percentile for the national sample), the first time in memory that a group of students from that school had manifested outstanding achievement. The mean score for the grade was at the national sample: 42nd percentile, compared with the 25th percentile two years before.

The fifth grades of the elementary schools included several teachers whose teachers were using the models of teaching regularly but at a mechanical level and several teachers whose regular use approached executive control. Again, the administration of the social-studies test from the ITBS battery permitted a comparison of achievement between the "mechanical use" and "executive control" classes.

When the distributions of scores are compared, the median student in the "executive control" classes is between the 85th and 90th percentiles of the "mechanical use" classes. Compared to national norms, the median student of the "executive control" classes was at the 76th percentile, compared to the 44th percentile for the "mechanical use" classes. The median "grade-equivalent" scores for the "executive control" classes range from 6.5 to 7.9, or from 0.7 to 2.1 above the national sample median. For the "mechanical use" classes, the range was from 5.0 to 6.1. The distributions of scores in the extreme classes — those whose students were in executive-use classes compared with mechanical-use classes, barely overlap, as can be seen in figure 2.1.

Mean scores in all these classes exceed the average scores for fifth grades in the district. However, the importance of reaching "executive control" is underlined by these data.

GENDER

River City has consistently found that males in the lower SES schools regularly achieve less than the females. By the eighth grade, the median female stands where the 69th percentile does, in standard test terms. *In executive-control classrooms, the distributions of males and females are roughly equivalent.* This finding is consistent with basic research on the models of teaching used in the River City program. Essentially, these models of teaching are blind to socioeconomic status, gender, race, and ethnicity.

ACHIEVEMENT IN CADRE-DISSEMINATED SCHOOLS

After faculties of the first three schools were trained by consultants, a cadre of teachers disseminated the teaching strategies to other schools in the district. Results for the first nine schools on the Iowa Test of Basic Skills were substantial. Each of the nine schools completed 8 tests for a total of 72 test scores. In grade-level-equivalent terms, 40 of the 72 scores reflected gains of greater than 4 months over the previous year's results, and 20 of the scores reflected gains of between 2 and 4 months. *It is important to note that faculties taught by a cadre of their peers learned new models of teaching as thoroughly, implemented them as frequently, and gained equally large student outcomes as faculties taught by outside consultants.*

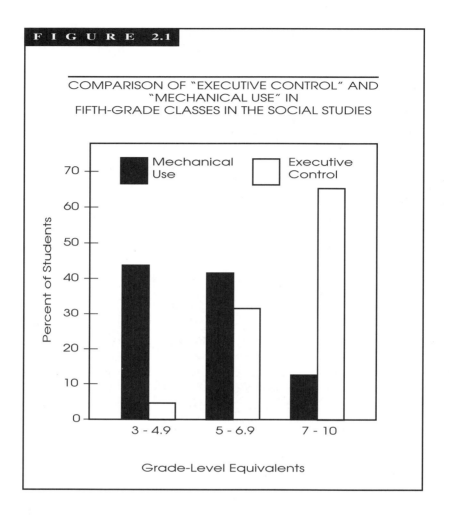

FIGURE 2.1

COMPARISON OF "EXECUTIVE CONTROL" AND
"MECHANICAL USE" IN
FIFTH-GRADE CLASSES IN THE SOCIAL STUDIES

SUMMARY

The River City Program focused on instruction, staff development, and organizing faculties for collaborative action. Schools entered the program as units. A condition was that 80 percent of each
faculty had voted to participate, and the majority decision was bind-
ing on the entire faculty. Within the program all teachers in each
participating school studied a set of well-tested models of teaching
selected to increase the learning capacity of their students. The
faculties were organized into study groups and elected councils
whose responsibility was to examine information about the health of

the school and plan school-improvement initiatives (Joyce, Murphy, Showers, and Murphy 1989).

In some River City schools, the need for school improvement was urgent. However, as the teachers learned to use models of teaching designed to increase cooperative activity, teach concepts, and teach students to work inductively and memorize information, the learning rates of the students improved dramatically.

As in the case of Success for All (Slavin and others 1990) and the Schenley Program (Wallace, Lemahieu, and Bickel 1990), large effects on student learning occurred rapidly in the first year of implementation, once again demonstrating the efficacy of school faculties that make changes in curriculum and instruction. Students responded right away to changes in instruction and began to accelerate their rates of learning in an educational environment that was designed to do just that: teach the students to be more powerful learners. Many educators believe that school-improvement efforts will not have demonstrable effects on students for several years, but the evidence points toward quite a different conclusion.

Now, let's move into our next setting, where individual, school, and district governance shape staff development efforts to improve student learning.

UNIVERSITY TOWN

The University Town program was structured around individual, school, and district levels of staff development. The program attempted to generate school cultures as centers of inquiry through:

- embedded time for colleagueship
- a system for shared decision-making
- an information-rich, formative study environment
- the study of research on curriculum and teaching
- a comprehensive staff development system

Comparatively speaking, University Town schools have traditionally manifested very high student achievement. Nearly all teachers and administrators were surprised to learn that they were able to generate annual increases in quality of writing several times over levels before the program was developed.

They were also surprised to learn that districtwide and schoolwide initiatives in curriculum and instruction generated more teacher satisfaction and more productivity than did individually governed staff development

CHAPTER 3

THE UNIVERSITY TOWN PROGRAM: EXPLORING GOVERNANCE STRUCTURES

BRUCE JOYCE, EMILY CALHOUN, NINA CARRAN,
JAY SIMSER, DALLAS RUST, AND CAL HALLIBURTON

> What happens when teachers are supported for individual, schoolwide, and districtwide efforts to improve student learning?

Proposals for school renewal come from three frames of reference that differ considerably in terms of who is pictured at the center of the process:

1. One puts the individual practitioner at the center.
2. The second places the school site at the center.
3. The third emphasizes the district office and districtwide initiatives in curriculum and instruction.

Each frame of reference has merit: individuals, schools, and districts can be sources of school renewal.

The Individual Practitioner as the Source. Teachers and principals deliver education. They have had to teach themselves most of what they know, borrowing ideas from their colleagues as they can. They are the most knowledgeable people about the problems they face. Yet, time to study and to develop actions to address these problems has not been built into their paid duties, and in most settings they get very little help from sources external to the school. Providing them with the resources and opportunities to strengthen their skills and help them carry out their work in a reflective, inquiring mode makes very good sense.

The School as the Source. While classrooms are the scene of instruction, the school as a whole needs to have a coherent program, for many aspects of schooling and school renewal cannot be changed by individuals working alone. The school climate and the curriculum can be incoherent unless there is a *faculty* in the real sense of the word, assessing the health of the school and making decisions about ways to make it better. Thus, we have the movement toward "site-based" approaches to school renewal and paradigms like "schoolwide action research" to help faculties improve student learning by inquiring into it.

District Initiatives as the Source. While classrooms and schools are the stage where the play of education is enacted, the need for curricular coherence, technological improvement, and equity for all students impels districts to make initiatives. Even with greatly weakened central-office personnel, curriculum guides continue to be written, computers are purchased, assessment systems developed, and ways of evaluating personnel and supervising them are adopted.

The district is the political unit for education and has the responsibility to view the schools and teachers with some objectivity and to generate ways of improving education. The technical rationale for district initiative depends to a large extent on the argument that the district unit can "see" things that may not be apparent to the school-based personnel and can marshal the resources for a quality of curriculum that may be beyond the development capability of the smaller units.

THE UNIVERSITY TOWN PROGRAM

The unusual feature of the University Town program is that this district of 11 schools, 350 teachers, and 5,000 students provided strong and balanced support for individual, school, and districtwide initiatives. Consequently, the University Town staff development program provided an opportunity to observe the effects of three governance options in terms of the types of objectives generated, the activities pursued, the implementation of innovations, and the effects on students. The 1992-93 academic year, when all three governance options were operating robustly, is the time frame of the experiences reported here.

The University Town program came about because administrators acknowledged the measures of "truth" underlying often-competing theses about school renewal and staff development—theses that provide rationale for all three governance modes.

The individual mode supports the energy of individuals. Renewal opportunities place the locus of control with the person, whose actions will presumably be congruent with that individual's perceptual world. Individually generated staff development acknowledges the division of the workplace into units (classrooms) where individual teachers use their perceptions and strengths to create innovations to which they can be committed.

Schoolwide action research is supported because the curricular and social-climate dimensions of the school can be addressed in a way not possible through individual or small-group action alone. Further, schoolwide action research directly addresses the goal of encouraging shared governance and increasing the capacity of the faculty to inquire into and solve problems requiring concerted, democratic action.

The districtwide initiatives emphasize the importance of curricular coherence and the development of district faculties who embrace professional citizenship in the larger sense of belonging to a community whose children deserve equity in educational opportunity and a common core of knowledge and skills.

The description of the program in the next section has been adapted from a memorandum to the district faculty in University Town in February 1992. This memorandum was accompanied by meetings with the district faculty to explain the rationale for the plan. Several passages have been modified to increase clarity for readers who are unfamiliar with the context and to provide information about background events.

THE DISTRICT AND THE SCHOOL AS A LEARNING CENTER FOR FACULTY AND STUDENTS

How do we proceed? We face a world where social change and technological advance will make curriculums and ways of teaching age far more rapidly than in the past. The result is that the quality of education of our children will increasingly depend on our own continuing self-education.

We need to build a setting where our study of what to teach and how to teach it are a regular part of our jobs—essentially to make schools learning centers for ourselves and for our students. Thus, we have, once again, to reach beyond what was regarded as normal and satisfactory in the recent past and create anew our study of curriculum and instruction.

In the past, school districts invested very little in opportunities for study by teachers or administrators. Curriculum committees did their work and new documents appeared. One or two days were set aside to think through the changes and learn the teaching strategies needed to use them. Brief workshops conveyed the ideas that were fashionable, and followup activities were often absent or haphazard.

We are now building conditions that will lay the base for far more stimulating conditions for professional life than those represented by traditional staff development practice. *The six conditions described below involve seeing ourselves in multiple roles and providing time and support for our individual and common work as educators.*

THREE PROFESSIONAL SPHERES

One concept guiding this effort involves seeing ourselves in three roles as professionals: one is as individual educators; another is as a member of a school faculty; and the third is as a member of the district faculty. These are our professional spheres of activity. In each sphere, we will study what we are doing and make initiatives for improving education. As a district, we support our efforts in each sphere by allocating resources, arranging time, and establishing structures that facilitate learning.

ON TIME AND COLLEAGUESHIP

One of our arrangements is for regular weekly time for faculties and study groups to meet. Every Wednesday, from 1:30 to 4:00 p.m., is set aside for developmental activities. Action-research plans can be made, study groups can focus effort on the language arts and learning strategies, and curriculum-planning committees can do their work without interrupting instructional time. The clear time for collaborative work over these areas should bring us closer together as a community of learners studying how our students can learn better.

SUPPORT FOR INDIVIDUALS

Under the Iowa Education Excellence Program, Phase III, the Individual Growth Fund has been set up. Teachers are able to select activities of their choice and receive support of up to $465 to defray the cost of the activities. Individuals will select activities according to the dictates of their professional judgment. (The state and local education associations were active in designing this initiative and persuading the state government to support it for all teachers in the state.)

SUPPORT FOR SCHOOL FACULTIES

Each school in University Town received a budget of $350 per faculty FTE to use for conducting schoolwide action research and to support the staff development needed for their initiatives. Thus, a school with 30 faculty members received $10,500 per annum to support their decisions. These funds, like those for teachers' individual growth, came from the Iowa Education Excellence Program designed to support school restructuring in Iowa.

Schools are asked to elect action-research facilitation teams and lead the faculties in the study of the school and the generation of initiatives to improve it. (Again, the teachers' organizations were active in the design of the initiative and the procurement of funding for it.) The classic action-research model—emphasizing the development of shared leadership, the collection of data relative to the health of the school, the generation of initiatives (one at a time) to improve aspects of student learning, the implementation of those initiatives, and the study of effects on students—will be used.

SUPPORT FOR DISTRICT-LEVEL INITIATIVES

The core of the content of the district initiative is an approach to the teaching of reading and writing that uses conceptual, constructivist models of teaching to make the reading/writing connection visible. In addition, the "Just Read" program (see chapter 6) will increase the amounts and quality of independent reading by students. Teacher/administrator coordination and support teams were formed to articulate the curriculum and to arrange support.

The two models of teaching selected for initial study are "inductive thinking in cooperative groups" and "concept attainment," both basic approaches to teach students to build concepts (Joyce, Weil, and Showers 1992). The district staff development will emphasize concepts that enhance reading comprehension and, through the reading-writing connection, skill in strategies for writing.

In all three spheres of governance, we will work together to implement the changes; the cadre (see below) will provide support; and the study-group structure will pull us through the struggle for thorough implementation.

ON LEARNING TOGETHER: A CADRE TO SUPPORT ALL SPHERES

Another effort that is under way is the organization of a cadre whose members will study curriculum, teaching, and school improvement. Teachers who represent a range of specialties form the cadre, and all principals are—by virtue of their leadership role in the school and district faculty—members. This group has been studying several models of teaching and has been working with the Just Read and Write initiatives.

For the long term, the cadre needs to have the capability to provide service to building leadership teams and faculties in each school. Its primary functions include providing leadership and training for school and district initiatives, developing materials and procedures to support learning at all levels and across all groups, and studying the effects of school and district actions. For example, the cadre will

1. provide training on generic teaching skills and a wide variety of models of teaching

2. provide training on the implementation of curriculum areas as content and processes are changed

3. build the capacity of leadership teams to organize the faculties into productive problem-solving teams, including the organization of study groups for the implementation of training in curriculum and instruction

4. develop training materials and procedures, including training for innovations that emerge as priorities

5. apply understanding of the change process to curricular and instructional innovation and help all personnel understand change

6. study implementation, and modify procedures accordingly, and facilitate the study by teachers of the effects on students

ON STUDY GROUPS AND COLLEAGUESHIP

All faculties have organized themselves into study groups. The study-group structure is intended to increase collegial interaction in the study of teaching and curriculum and, especially, to facilitate the implementation of teaching strategies and curriculum changes. Each faculty has organized a group of action-research facilitators. These individuals will work with the district's action-research consultants to study the action-research process and how to lead it. (This is the end of the memorandum that described features of the program to district faculty.)

Extensive discussions were conducted in the district and within school faculties around the concepts in the above document, and then the program commenced.

The cadre of teachers and the principals of the schools received training on teaching strategies, the reading/writing connections, and the processes of offering staff development and consultation to their colleagues. School leadership teams and faculties studied how to conduct action research. Principals studied the development of school-renewal efforts and action research. The language arts team, cadre, and teachers studied the teaching of reading and writing, and they settled on the use of models of teaching to make the reading-writing connection visible to students.

Consultants worked with faculties until the cadre was ready to assume that role. In all areas, the consultants were to "work their way out of business" as cadre members gained the confidence to step into the support role.

Because of the results of the early phases of the formative-evaluation studies and the indications from research on reading and writing of the central role of expository prose in language development, expository prose received the greatest attention in the teaching of both reading and writing.

DESIGN OF THE STUDIES

In a real sense, the entire program was conducted as districtwide action research, with schoolwide action research and the inquiry of individuals and small groups nested therein. The formative-evaluation component was designed to obtain multiple sources of information about reactions to, implementation of, and effects of initiatives from each governance source. The three parts of the formative-evaluation studies consisted of an interview study, an ethnographic study, and a formal study of the quality of writing.

1. *The interview study was designed to explore the perspectives of teachers about the individual initiatives, the schoolwide initiatives, and the district initiatives.*

The perspectives of teachers about the effects of these initiatives on themselves, about the degrees of implementation, and about the effects on students were obtained through interviews with a sample of teachers in each of the elementary schools ("The Teacher Satisfaction and Productivity Interview"). Content analyses were made of the responses to the open-ended items. In addition, on a biweekly basis, individual teachers filled out an open-ended log asking for their perceptions of implementation and their identification of needs for support.

2. *In the ethnographic study, onsite participant-observation was oriented toward the dynamics of action research around school and district initiatives.*

One of the consultants spent over 60 days in residence during the year. The consultant was responsible for supporting the action-research facilitation teams and providing service to school faculties, cadre, and policy-makers on the language arts and models of teaching component. In addition, the consultant was responsible for studying progress in the action-research and models of teaching/language arts initiative. She obtained the perspectives of principals, leadership teams, and central-office personnel through interviews and observations of meetings. She conducted formal and informal discussions with teams, study groups, and individuals.

Quantitative data were obtained through records of implementation of program components, including examination of the logs of use, records of student reading, action-research plans, and observations of teaching. The problems inherent in combining the support and observational roles were counterbalanced by (1) the access to the process, (2) the additional quantitative data, (3) the comparison of results with those of the other components of the inquiry process, and (4) the comparison with a smaller qualitative study conducted by one of the teachers in the district.

3. *The formal study of quality of writing was designed to provide an indication of student learning needs.*

Writing was selected because it is a goal of all the curriculum areas at all levels and is probably influenced by more areas of instruction than any other aspect of academic learning. Diagnostic information from the study of writing has implications for all the curriculum areas and levels. Also, it has been, nationwide, an extremely difficult area to improve—a tough bottom line and one worth pursuing as a district.

Samples of expository, persuasive, and narrative writing were collected from all students in grades 4, 6, and 8 at the beginning and end of the 1992-93 school year. Those samples were submitted to a content analysis, and the differences between the fall and spring scores were compared to a baseline obtained in University Town the prior year and compared to the annual national changes estimated from the National Assessment of Writing Progress.

The remainder of this school-renewal story is organized around what we learned from the interview study, the ethnographic study, and the quality-of-writing study. Our written presentation may make these studies appear as disparate inquiries, but like any complex storyline, they were dynamically intertwined.

We will begin with the perceptions of the teachers and the ethnographers about the reception and implementation of the three components of the program and then discuss the study of quality of writing.

THE INTERVIEW STUDY: TEACHER SATISFACTION AND PRODUCTIVITY

These interviews were designed to explore teachers' perceptions of the content of the three initiatives (individual, school, and district) and the satisfaction and productivity that emerged from each of them. Thirty-five questions were asked about the initiatives. Teachers' general perceptions were also solicited through open-ended invitations interspersed throughout the interviews.

The data presented below are taken from one round of interviews conducted between May 17 and June 7, 1993. The interviews lasted from about 15 minutes to 2 hours. Four persons conducted them: two consultants from outside the district, one teacher who is past president of the teachers' association, and one representative of the central office. The results did not differ by interviewer.

SAMPLE

Sixty-four teachers were interviewed in the May-June 1993 round. A random sample of teachers was drawn from the faculties of each of the nine elementary schools (from five to eight per school depending on faculty size). Altogether there were 163 full-time teachers assigned to classrooms and support roles in these nine schools. Thus, 39 percent of the classroom teachers were interviewed. The 64 teachers represented a wide range of years of teaching experience. There was one first-year teacher and one 36-year veteran, with the rest distributed as shown below in table 3.1.

Twenty-five teachers received their bachelor's degrees from the University in the town the district is located in. Nineteen others received their undergraduate education at other universities or colleges within the state. Ten others were educated elsewhere in the adjacent Midwestern states. The other 10 were undergraduates at institutions scattered from coast to coast. Thirty-three of those interviewed have master's degrees and three hold doctorates. Nearly all expect to continue teaching until retirement. Three expressed aspirations to become administrators and five to become staff development or curriculum specialists.

INFORMATION GAINED/RESULTS

We have organized what we learned around three topics:

1. teachers' *perceptions of satisfaction* across the three sources of initiatives
2. teachers' *perceptions of changes in the classroom and effects on students*

TABLE   3.1

YEARS OF TEACHING EXPERIENCE

Years	Number
1-5	5
6-10	9
11-15	17
16-20	15
21-25	7
26-30	5
31-36	5
NA	1

Note: The distribution approximates that of the entire staff of the elementary schools.

3. *impressions* about the introduction, reception, implementation, and effectiveness of each level of initiative

---

PERCEPTIONS OF SATISFACTION: CROSS-INITIATIVE COMPARISONS

The interview schedule asked the 64 teachers to discuss each program component in detail. For cross-initiative comparisons, the critical items were four questions tapping teachers' estimates of the worth of each initiative: the Individual Growth Fund Initiative (IGF), the Schoolwide Action Research Initiative (AR), and the district Models of Teaching/Language Arts Initiative (MOT/LA). These parallel items asked them whether the initiative should be continued in University Town, whether they would recommend it to another school district, whether there were positive effects for students, and what their general feelings about the initiative were.

To interpret the results shared below, it is important to know that 12.5 percent of the sample did not make use of the Individual Growth Fund (IGF) Initiative at all and that 18.5 percent used the IGF money to develop instructional plans or materials and thus did not use the resources for staff development. Another 18.5 percent had not used the IGF when the interviews were conducted but planned to use it in the summer (most did).

Question: Should the initiative be continued?

Table 3.2 contains the responses to the questions about continuing each initiative. Clearly, the majority of these teachers favored the continuance of all three initiatives. The largest percentage favored continuing the Models of Teaching/Language Arts Initiative. The next largest favored the continuance of the Schoolwide Action Research Initiative.

Question: Would you recommend the initiative to another district?

Table 3.3 displays the responses. Again, the majority of these teachers would recommend each of the initiatives to persons working in other districts. The differences favoring the Models of Teaching/Language Arts and Schoolwide Action Research Initiatives were similar to the responses to the question asking whether the initiatives should be continued.

Question: Did the initiative have an effect on students?

Table 3.4 displays the responses to this question. The results closely approximated those of the other two questions designed to

T A B L E   3.2

SATISFACTION/PRODUCTIVITY INTERVIEWS
COMPARISON OF INITIATIVES: SHOULD THE INITIATIVE BE CONTINUED?

Initiative	Yes	No	Don't Know or No Comment	Total
	N (%)	N (%)	N	
IGF	38 (59.4%)	4 (6.3%)	22 (34.4%)	64
ACTION RES.	49 (78.4%)	3 (4.7%)	12 (18.7%)	64
MODELS/LA	61 (95.3%)	1 (1.6%)	2 (3.1%)	64

T A B L E   3.3

SATISFACTION/PRODUCTIVITY INTERVIEWS
CROSS-INITIATIVE COMPARISON: RECOMMEND TO ANOTHER DISTRICT (PERSON)?

Initiative	Yes	No	Unsure, Missing, or No Comment
	N (%)	N (%)	N (%)
IGF	36 (56.3%)	0	28 (43.7%)
ACTION RES.	50 (76.6%)	3 (4.7%)	9 (14.1%)
MODELS/LA	56 (87.5%)	3 (4.7%)	5 (7.8%)

T A B L E   3.4

SATISFACTION/PRODUCTIVITY INTERVIEWS
CROSS-INITIATIVE COMPARISON: PERCEPTIONS OF EFFECTS ON STUDENTS

Initiative	Yes	No	Unsure	Missing or NC
	N (%)	N (%)	N (%)	N (%)
IGF	35 (54.7%)	1 (1.6%)	2 (3.1%)	26 (40.6%)
ACTION RES.	48 (75%)	8 (12.5%)	2 (3.2)	6 (9.4%)
MODELS/LA	54 (84.4%)	3 (4.7%)	2 (3.1%)	4 (6.3%)

T A B L E 3.5				
SATISFACTION-PRODUCTIVITY INTERVIEWS: "HOW DO YOU FEEL ABOUT ...?"				
Initiative	*Good/O.K.*	*Indifferent*	*Worse*	*Missing*
	N (%)	N (%)	N (%)	N (%)
IGF	41 (61.4%)	1 (1.6%)	0	22 (34.4%)
ACTION RES.	51 (79.3%)	8 (12.5%)	1 (1.6%)	4 (6.3%)
LA/MOT	61 (95.3%)	0	1 (1.6%)	2 (3.1%)

obtain an assessment of the teachers' general perceptions of the three initiatives.

Question: How do you feel about ......?

Table 3.5 contains the results on teachers' feelings about each initiative. The results are in line with those from the other three questions. Again, the two collective components were apparently viewed very positively, and the Individual Growth Fund Initiative was viewed as positive in terms of general feeling by three out of five persons.

Experience in Teaching and Academic Background as Factors Affecting Responses to the Components. Cross-tabulations were made between years of teaching experience and the four variables with respect to each initiative, and chi-square values were computed. In no case did years of teaching experience appear to affect response to the questions exploring reactions to any of the three components of the program. Apparently, the responses were independent of the amounts of teaching experience of the respondents. Similar computations were made to explore whether the location of colleges attended were influential, and the findings were identical to those exploring experience as a possible factor.

Consistency of Response. Cross-tabulations were made to determine the consistency of responses within and across initiatives. There was great consistency. For example, just two of the persons who reported good or excellent feelings toward the Models of Teaching/Language Arts Initiative indicated that it should not be continued, and just one indicated that it should not be continued in University Town. The picture was similar with respect to the Schoolwide Action Research Initiative. Only 4 of the 42 who indicated good feelings about it thought it had had no effects on students. Three of the five who indicated poor feelings thought it had had no effect on students. With respect to the Individual Growth Fund, where 41 teachers indicated positive feelings, 33 thought it had benefitted students.

Summary of Teachers' Satisfaction Across the Initiatives. These findings are pertinent to the current theses on staff development pertaining to individual motivation, "buy in," and the role of district-office staff in generating initiatives. In the case of University Town, the perceptions of the teachers suggest that the districtwide initiative was regarded positively by nearly all the teachers, and the schoolwide action research, which is inherently complicated socially, enjoyed positive regard by nearly as many interviewees. The Individual Growth Fund, while supported by about half of the teachers, was responded to equivocally by the other half.

These results of the comparison of responses to the three sources of initiatives are somewhat different from what many might expect. The virtually unanimous approval of the district initiative and the considerable support for the schoolwide action research stand out boldly, but the real curiosity is the large number of persons who did not express direct and positive support for the individual initiative. It is puzzling that one teacher in eight did not use the IGF at all. It is less puzzling that one in five teachers used the funding for preparation. However, it is surprising that so many did not answer positively that the initiative should be continued or recommended. Also, nearly all of those who did not use it or comment on it were very positive toward the other initiatives.

This information challenges current opinions held by many staff development specialists that staff development tailored to the individual will have the greatest approval and that staff development around district initiatives, even when selected with broad teacher participation, will nonetheless be regarded as imposed and will be rejected because its impetus was "top down" instead of "bottom-up."

PERCEPTIONS OF CHANGES IN CLASSROOMS AND EFFECTS ON STUDENT LEARNING

Open-ended questions enabled the teachers to use their own descriptions and labels to describe what had happened or was happening and their feelings about these experiences. Generally, they described changes in instruction, in students, in materials, and in effects on themselves, including their morale. Overall, specific and positive changes were mentioned:

- for the Individual Growth Fund Initiative by 26 teachers

- for the Action Research Initiative by 39 teachers
- for the Models of Teaching/Language Arts Initiative by 58 teachers.

Thirty-nine teachers mentioned specific and positive changes attributable to the Schoolwide Action Research Initiative, 17 did not mention a change attributable to the Action-Research Initiative, and 8 believed there had been a negative effect without identifying what that negative effect was.

Fifty-eight teachers mentioned a particular positive effect of the Models of Teaching/Language Arts Initiative, while six teachers indicated that it had produced a negative effect (four of these interviewees also attributed negative effects to the Schoolwide Action Research Initiative). Not surprisingly, given the results reported above, 28 teachers did not mention positive effects from the Individual Growth Fund Initiative, but then no one mentioned negative effects from the IGF either.

Another open-ended question solicited perceptions of the effects of the initiatives on students. Positive effects on students were mentioned:

- for the Individual Growth Fund Initiative by 35 teachers (54.7 percent)
- for the Action Research Initiative by 48 teachers (75.0 percent)
- for the Models of Teaching/Language Arts Initiative by 54 teachers (84.4 percent)

These responses were consistent with those on general opinions about the initiatives.

The interview guides were structured to elicit from teachers reasonably concrete and specific details, and we will now turn to the results of that set of queries.

IMPRESSIONS ACROSS INITIATIVES

The Individual Growth Fund Initiative: Detailed Impressions. The set of questions related to the IGF were designed to explore what individuals did with their funds, whether there was a subsequent impact on the classroom environment, and what specific influences the initiative had on student learning. The questions also were used to follow up on specifics that interviewees had mentioned about an initiative.

Six teachers used the resources to defray the expenses of taking a university course. Eighteen (28.1 percent) attended conferences. Twenty-one (32 percent) attended a workshop or series of workshops. The others, as described earlier, made preparation for teaching through planning or the making of instructional materials or did not use the funds.

Credentials and graduate credit influenced only four persons in their choice of options. About one-fourth reported that district initiatives influenced their choices. The influence of other teachers was mentioned rarely.

Teachers had a hard time pinning down changes as a result of their Individual Growth Fund experiences. About half of the interviewees reported that the experience was congruent with the goal they had in mind when making the decision about what to do with their growth-fund money. Most of the others were noncommittal about goal congruence. Many responded vaguely to the general question "What happened as a result of your experience?" Ten interviewees mentioned the production or introduction of instructional materials, but many made vague or general comments. Asked about specific differences in their classrooms, 13 (20.3 percent) were able to identify particular changes in instruction or materials; several mentioned changes in students but couldn't specify the cause of the change. The remainder were unspecific or mentioned nothing, and four said that there had been no effect. With respect to specific effects on student learning, of the 35 who said there had been positive effects, only 14 teachers could pin down or cite a specific effect.

Overall, most of the teachers who used their funds for staff development liked the Individual Growth Fund Initiative, and many of these teachers appeared to have reasonably clear purposes, tried to select options that would pay off, and felt the component was, for them, relatively satisfying and productive. However, many of the users had difficulty providing specific information. For them, it was a personal experience and communicating about it was relatively difficult.

The Schoolwide Action-Research Initiative: Detailed Impressions. The Action-Research Initiative had been in full swing for about a year when the round of interviews occurred, though planning meetings had been held the year before (1991-92). By that time all the faculties had been working their way toward shared decision-making, making agreements about what to study, trying to generate initiatives, and learning to study the effects of their initiatives. The tasks for the 1992-93 year were to select a common initiative; implement it, including arranging for staff development and studying their implementation data; and study the effects on students. Time during the "shortened day" schedule was set aside for meetings to make the decisions, work on implementation, and study effects.

Action research was selected by district and school representatives because of its structured approach to collective study and its use of collaborative action for school renewal. Action research was presented to faculties as disciplined inquiry focused on improving student learning. The value gained from conducting action research was to be determined by each faculty, whose members identify a common goal, how best to achieve it, and how to assess its attainment. Creating faculty synergy for collective study and action was seen as a key element in creating learning communities in each school and in the district as a whole. Thus, a major component of action research was the development of a collegial decision-making organization in each school, including facilitation teams, study teams, and mechanisms for democratic decision-making on major issues. These school faculties were trying to learn how to study student learning and how to generate initiatives that fit the needs of their sites.

Specific interview questions were designed to obtain teachers' perceptions about the purposes of action research, about what had been accomplished through the action-research process, and about how individuals felt about schoolwide action research. When examining the responses to the four questions below, it may be helpful to consider that a major impetus for the action-research component came from the state teachers' organization, which offered some fiscal support and contributed much moral support for the initiative.

Question: Why do you think the district moved into the area of schoolwide action research?

Nearly half (30) the teachers indicated that it was an attempt by the central office to develop greater control over and accountability for the schools. Fifteen teachers mentioned increased collaboration in research activity. Six teachers focused on benefits to the students as the goal. Four teachers said it was being used because it was "trendy"; one said it was being used because it would make the teachers work harder; and eight said they simply did not know why the district was interested in schoolwide action research. The responses of two-thirds were at variance with the purpose articulated by the planners, as, for example, in the memorandum* that was used in the orientation of the faculties to the purpose and structure of all the components.

Question: Describe the action-research goal in your building.

Responses to this item were compared with the written statements of objectives and initiatives that had been approved by vote in each of the schools as the faculties worked their way through the action-research process.

Twenty-nine teachers (45.3 percent) described the goal in terms consistent with the goal adopted in their schoolwide action-research plan. Eighteen (28.1 percent) described a goal not in the action-research plan. Eight said they did not know what the goal was; eight made negative comments about the process, without mentioning a goal; and one didn't comment.

Question: What happened in your school as a result of action research?

Consistent with the responses to the questions designed to elicit general impressions, 48 teachers (75 percent) mentioned better learning opportunities for the students and closer colleagueship with other teachers. There is an interesting contrast here: in response to an earlier question, about half of these 48 teachers had mentioned "greater control by the administration" as the overall purpose of schoolwide action research. Eight teachers mentioned negative things, largely that colleagueship had been reduced by the effort, and eight responded in vague generalities.

Question: What happened in your classroom as a result of action research?

About three-fifths of the teachers (62 percent) thought there had been positive effects in their classrooms from schoolwide action research, and the others felt there had been no changes or negative changes. Positive effects on instructional materials (17), teaching strategies (11), and students (11) were mentioned most frequently. Fifteen teachers (23.4 percent) reported that there had been no change, and 9 (14 percent) made negative comments about the effects of the initiative on the classroom, which appeared to be a halo from their generally negative feelings toward the initiative.

All teachers were asked to participate in making the decisions about the direction for the schoolwide initiative. Most school faculties used an 80 percent majority as the decision-making point, and the

---

* A modified version of this memorandum provided the text for the above section "The District and the School as a Learning Center for Faculty and Students," beginning on page 55.

facilitation teams strived for a consensus by all members of the faculty.

Between-school variance. With respect to these questions about schoolwide action research, there was considerable variance in the responses of the faculties from different schools. In one school, all the respondents indicated that the purpose was to help students learn more and/or to generate greater collegiality. In that same school, the responses about the action plans were consistent with the written action plans, and all teachers mentioned changes in the classrooms and specific effects on students.

In the school where the most contrast was present, most respondents were unclear about the purpose, the school initiative, or the effects. Yet, that school faculty had actually *done* something—found a focus for study, gathered and shared some information, and were considering actions to take.

Summary: Perceptions of specific aspects of the action-research initiative. As indicated above, most of the teachers expressed positive feelings and believed that worthwhile changes were taking place as a result of their work with schoolwide action research. However, a certain number of teachers had mixed or even negative responses. The fact that so many were not clear about the action-research plans is interesting, for those plans were arrived at through collective study and action and were very public throughout the schools, both in written form and in oral declarations. The vague responses offered by many interviewees when details and examples were sought is also interesting.

Despite feelings among a majority of the sample of increased collegiality and perceptions of positive effects on classroom practice and on students' behaviors/attitudes, a significant amount of confusion and some resistance remain around schoolwide action research in University Town. Nevertheless, compared to many faculties attempting to use schoolwide action research, these schools are making considerable progress.

Some of the comments from the end-of-year reports prepared by one of the external consultants are relevant to the progress the 11 school faculties (including middle school and high school) made in using schoolwide action research:

> In the University Town Schools, all eleven faculties learned something this year about conducting action research. How useful this learning was and its degree of direct impact on student learning varied from school to school. Thanks to the coordinator and a local consultant, plus the tremendous time commitment of

many facilitators, the technical and social dimensions of conducting action research improved in most schools: establishing a
common goal, collecting and organizing data, and taking action
indicated by the goal and by the data being collected.

Eight school faculties were able to keep the focus on student
achievement a dominant factor in their action research. This may
sound like a given considering the Phase III goal, but it is
extremely rare in school-based improvement efforts (David and
Peterson 1984, Calhoun 1992, Muncey and McQuillan 1993). In
one three-year study of school faculties engaging in schoolwide
action research in another setting, only about one-fourth of the
schools were able to establish a common student-learning goal
during their first year; about one-fourth more the second year,
about one-fourth more the third year; and the rest gave up or
continue to set goals in areas peripheral to student learning. Only
about half of those that established a student learning goal actually made an initiative in curriculum or instruction and studied its
effects.

This year, seven of the nine faculties collected schoolwide
student behavioral data of one or more types. This is in sharp
contrast to the predominance of perceptual data, or in some cases
no data, collected during the first year. Faculty-wide study of
professional literature around their goal at five schools appeared
to provide some faculties with more options and actions to take in
pursuing their goal.

Based on meetings with facilitator teams and on the end-of-
year reports prepared by each school facilitator team, seven
school faculties know more about the achievement of their students now than they did ten months ago. This is especially true in
the area of writing in three schools, and in technology, vocabulary, and reading comprehension in other schools. What these
faculties learned as communities about student learning and
progress may be the most important results of schoolwide action
research thus far.

Two elementary school faculties made particular progress
this year in working together to develop common goals in schools
where many members had been heavily invested in individualistic efforts and where role relationships changed as facilitation
teams created shared governance processes that had not existed
before. The facilitators, teachers, and school administrator in
those buildings persisted until they had virtually unanimous
agreement on common goals.

Six of the eleven school faculties have reached a stage of progress in action research greater than that in any previously reported study of schoolwide action research, with several of the faculties generating initiatives in curriculum and instruction and proceeding to implement them. Differences between schools appear to be partially due to the cohesiveness of the facilitation teams at the schools and to the ability of those teams to ensure that the faculty as a whole are continuously aware of objective data about student learning, are provided with sustained staff development to support their initiative, and attend to the implementation of agreed-on initiatives.

The notes of the consultant/participant observer are relatively congruent with the results from the interviews. However, the interviews revealed that, except in two of the schools, there were teachers who were, after two years, still confused about the purposes of action research in general and about the process in their schools. It appears that faculties can select initiatives—after studying their onsite data and considering several options for action and best practice—organize and participate in staff development relative to those options, study implementation and effects on students, and *still* find that some of their staff members are confused about the action-research process.

Considerable energy has to be invested in developing shared cognitions about the process if it is to continue to be satisfying and, in the long run, continued. An oddity (possibly political in essence) was the finding that nearly half of the teachers characterized schoolwide action research as manifesting intentions of control by the central office, whereas the teachers' organization had taken a leading role in choosing action research as a vehicle for Iowa's Phase III school improvement because of the degree of control it provides teachers over the selection of specific initiatives. One of the participants commented, "It may be that if you perceive yourself as a powerless slave, you will wear imaginary chains even after you have been made legally free."

The Models of Teaching/Language Arts Initiative: Detailed Impressions. The content of the district initiative emphasized the two models of teaching, concept attainment and inductive thinking in cooperative groups, and the reading-writing connection. The models were used to help students analyze literature and discover the strategies writers use to communicate (such as how expert writers introduce characters) and then help the students apply those strategies in their writing.

Teacher Perceptions of the Purpose, Impact, and Satisfaction Generated by the Models of Teaching/Language Arts Initiative. These questions about the Models of Teaching/Language Arts Initiative were similar to those asked about the Individual Growth Fund and the Schoolwide Action Research Initiatives: they focused on purpose, impact, and effects. The series of questions began with understandings about the rationale behind the initiative.

Question: Why do you think the district moved toward Integrated Language Arts using the Inductive and Concept-Attainment Strategies?

Most commonly mentioned reasons were

- to promote thinking skills (10 teachers, 15.6 percent)
- to improve curriculum and instruction (18 teachers, 27.9 percent)
- to try to reach all students (10 teachers, 15.6 percent)

Twelve teachers (18.8 percent) said the initiative was taken because of a research interest by personnel in the district office. The presence of extensive formative evaluation apparently led some teachers to wonder if they were participating in "someone's study" rather than participating in a process that contained embedded assessment to guide immediate and future school and district actions.

Seven teachers (10.9 percent) said they were unsure about the purpose. Seven teachers (10.9 percent) made vague and general comments that could not be classified.

Question: What has happened in your school as a result of the Models of Teaching/Language Arts Initiative?

Forty-three teachers (67.2 percent) mentioned wholly positive items, including increased collaboration among teachers (24 persons) and improved instruction (13 persons). Seven teachers (10.9 percent) mentioned negative items, all having to do with the collaborative process. Fourteen (21.9 percent) mentioned both positive and negative items with respect to collaboration and instruction.

Question: Are there changes in your classroom?

All but four teachers mentioned positive changes in materials, students, themselves, and student learning. Twenty-one teachers singled out materials as a major change. Four mentioned changes they believed were negative in impact, chiefly that the teaching strategies (the inductive and concept-attainment models) were mismatched with the students.

Question: How do you feel about the Models of Teaching?

Fifty-nine of the 64 teachers in the sample said they felt "Good" or "O.K." about both the inductive and concept-attainment models.

Missing data accounted for four of the five others. One felt "OK" about one model and "Worse" about the other.

Summary of Perceptions: The Models of Teaching/Language Arts Component. Curricular and instructional improvement to raise student learning was the goal of the policy-makers, and it is interesting that not all the teachers were clear about that, given the constant reiteration of the purpose and the continuous training in the language arts and models of teaching. However, the teaching and curricular content were well received by most teachers and believed to affect the students positively.

The following notes by one of the external consultants speak to the implementation of the inductive and concept-attainment models of teaching and to changes in language arts curriculum and instruction.

Implementation of Models of Teaching. Logs filled out weekly by the teachers, corroborated by observations and interviews, indicate that the use of Models of Teaching has increased substantially since last fall. The current mean use per teacher for April for the nine elementary schools was approximately 4.2 inductive lessons per week and 3.2 concept attainment lessons per week, with school means per teacher for the combination of models ranging from 2 to 6 lessons per week. *The use is sufficient to produce some effects on student achievement, although it has not yet reached the level that generates the large gains that are possible with mature implementation.* You may need to alter the configuration of support for the schools where use is lowest.

Implementation of the Curriculum. Progress continues to be made in implementing an integrated language arts curriculum in grades kindergarten through 6. Members of the Language Arts Cabinet and many members of the Models of Teaching Cadre continued their concentrated efforts to move forward in language arts: they conducted staff development sessions, made videotapes, shared with parents and community members the procedures and operations of the language arts program, and held formal and informal problem solving sessions. All this while they carried out their duties as teachers and principals.

To get a closer look at curriculum and instruction as it exists in the reality of the classroom, I observed 97 teaching/learning episodes in 49 of the 112 elementary classrooms, concentrating on the language arts and the use of the models of teaching. My frame of reference for these classroom visits was the study of teaching and the nature of the classroom instructional environment created for students. The data collected across classrooms included number of students present, curriculum content, materials used, nature of instruction, and how students were organized for instruction.

Students Present. The average number of students present in each classroom, excluding the five special needs and three pre-primary classrooms, was 20 (actually 20.4).

Curriculum Content. What follows is a list of the dominant academic content students were experiencing during my observations:

-48   language arts teaching/learning episodes

  2   lessons concentrated on spelling

14   lessons concentrated on reading

22   lessons combined reading and writing, or activities that integrated reading, writing, listening, and speaking

-12   interrelated teaching/learning episodes; examples were combinations of mathematics and writing; mathematics and literature; science, mathematics, and social studies

-11   mathematics teaching/learning episodes

 -8   science teaching/learning episodes

 -6   social studies teaching/learning episodes

-12   miscellaneous examples were all students at individual centers such as sand tables, blocks, art; Plan-Do-Review times; general review of the week

Materials Used. The primary instructional materials being used for language arts were, in descending order of frequency, trade books for independent and group reading, students' writing journals, commercial worksheets, and materials created by teachers or students (such as graphs, learning games, and data sets from literature).

During the mathematics episodes two primary source materials were being used: worksheets were most common followed by materials created by students and teachers. I observed several lessons in which students were organizing data and developing graphs; classifying data, forming sets, describing sets; classifying fractions and relating them to real-life applications. In both science and social studies, the most common materials used were projects students were developing, then textbooks and worksheets.

Nature of Instruction. The nature of the most common activities observed in language arts were, in descending order of frequency, students writing in journals and/or as part of Writers Workshop; students independent reading of tradebooks, magazines, and newspapers; and teachers reading aloud to students from classics. The most common group instruction observed across classrooms was the Daily Oral Language (DOL) lesson. I observed five inductive lessons (language arts, mathematics, and science) and two concept attainment lessons (language arts). I observed several interrelated lessons in which teachers had structured the activities so students were required to use skills from language arts, science, social studies, and mathematics, in cooperative groups, to accomplish their lesson tasks.

Social Organization of Students. Thirty-five of these 97 teaching/learning episodes were predominantly total-class groups; twenty-two had students working independently; nine had students organized into small groups of two to eight; and six had students organized into formal cooperative learning groups. The other twenty-five episodes were a combination of total class, independent, and/or small group.

The Implementation of Just Read. The purpose of "Just Read" is to help develop a society of habitual readers, thus increasing self-educating capacity. A related purpose is to increase the amount of education students receive through reading—ensuring that students read hundreds of books while in school. In addition, reading is an avenue for improving writing. Finally, reading independently is the surest way to consolidate the skills acquired through instruction, and skilled readers acquire vocabulary at a good rate if they read habitually, leading to the ability for more and more complex self-education.

There is enough data in the district records to make rough estimates of the program thus far. Judging from the weeks and months for which there were complete data, the approximately 3,000 University Town elementary students read about 300,000 books in each of the last two years, or an average of about 100 books per child each year. The K-2 students read (or were read to, in the case of pre-readers) the most, with an average of about 150 books per student per year. The grade 3-4 students read about 60 books per year, and the grade 4-5 students about 45 books per year on the average.

Variance among schools is significant, with the students in the three schools with the best implementations reading about twice the number of books of the schools with the lesser implementations (still far above the national average). During the 1992-1993 school year, several of the schools tailed off somewhat, but one school increased the average to about eight books per week per child. That school, incidentally, serves the lowest socio-economic level students in the district.

It has been demonstrated that the initiative can be implemented successfully in University Town, and Just Read represents a significant aspect of education for students. Different levels of implementation have created conditions of inequity, however, and the district needs to consider taking steps to ensure that the current gap, where students in one school are reading four times as much at home as students in some others, is not perpetuated.

The Study of the Reading/Writing Connection. More teachers are developing lessons in writing and in reading comprehension that relate to how authors craft a piece and how they develop and unify a piece. Staff interest in the specifics of teaching students to own our language as a powerful tool increased as the year progressed. For example, the number of questions about how to teach integrated lessons and how to help students focus and organize a piece of writing increased steadily during the year, as did the number of questions about how to connect the inductive and concept attainment models more fully to the conceptual base of the language arts.

THE STUDY OF QUALITY OF WRITING

This study of writing in University Town is an example of "districtwide action research." It concentrated on comparing samples of writing for grades 4, 6, and 8 from the early fall of 1992 and the late spring of 1993 in expository, persuasive, and narrative genres.

Writing was selected as the focus for the study for a variety of reasons, despite the fact that the study of writing is technically demanding and exceptionally labor intensive. Because American schools have had great difficulty affecting the development of competence in writing, quality of writing represents a severe test for a school-improvement program. In terms of the capability of the district faculty to increase student learning, we are fairly certain that if it knows it can increase competence in writing, then the faculty can have confidence that it can have success in any other curriculum area.

The efforts in the implementation of the language arts curriculum, the study of models of teaching that can further the reading-
writing connection, the Just Read program, and the action-research
program all can theoretically contribute to improvement in quality of
writing. This study was designed to explore whether improvement
occurred, not to attribute effort to a particular move or program.
Although the concentration of the initiative was on expository writing, the other genre were also examined to determine whether any
improvement in expository writing transferred to those types of
writing.

The design and results of the National Assessment of Educational
Progress provide a meaningful backdrop for the present study. The
national study provides information about the general progress made
by students between the 4th and 12th grades, and aspects of these
findings can be used as a basis for comparison with the situation in
University Town. Also, the National Assessment employs a system
for analyzing competence in writing that can be applied across the
grades, permitting year-to-year comparisons to be made. The National Assessment and the present study used instruments that are
comparable and were derived from similar sources.

Among its other findings, the National Assessment discovered
that progress in quality of writing is gradual, to say the least (Applebee
and others 1990, Applebee and others 1994). The average score of the
8th-grade students was at the 67th percentile of the 4th-grade distribution, and the average score of the 12th-grade students is at about
the 80th percentile of the 4th-grade students. Roughly speaking, there
is an average annual gain of about 3.5 percentile points. In "effect
size" terms, the average year-to-year gain is about 0.10, which translates to about 3.5 percentile-points per annum at the mean of a normal
distribution. Probably the gain is little more, if any, than developmental. The finding illustrates the difficulty American schools have had
in improving the quality of written composition. An unnerving finding from the National Assessment is that there is a serious gender
difference that widens over the grades. By the 12th grade, the median
score for males is at the 32nd percentile of the female distribution.

Judging from the results of the analyses conducted during the
1991-92 school year of writing samples collected from all the
fourth-, sixth-, and eighth-grade students, the children in the University Town schools have been progressing at an effect-size rate of
about .14, or almost half-again the national average. This translates to
a gain, at the mean, of about five percentile points. Thus, in 1991-92
the average 6th-grade student on the dimension "Focus and Organi-

zation" was at about the 60th percentile of the 4th-grade distribution. Year-to-year differences on the other two dimensions of the scale appear to be similar. Essentially, because the differences accumulate year-to-year, a student who began the 4th grade at the 50th percentile of the national average would graduate from the 12th grade well above the highest scoring 4th-grade student, whereas a counterpart in an average United States district would end up at the 80th percentile of the 4th-grade distribution.

DESIGN OF THE WRITING STUDY

This study, by collecting samples in fall 1992 (last week of September) and spring 1993 (last week of April/first week of May), was designed to learn whether changes occurred during the year and, if so, of what magnitude, compared to the baseline and to the National Assessment results.

Stimuli and Prompts for Writing. Standard prompts to elicit writing in the expository, persuasive, and narrative genre were presented to all fourth- and sixth-grade students in each elementary school. The stimuli were presented in written form, although, in the expository domain, the students observed visually the subjects they were to write about (a tree, the media center). Thirty minutes were allotted for responses after pilots indicated that virtually every student would complete the tasks within that period and scores of quality would not be affected by scheduling a longer period.

Sample Size and Selection. All the fourth-, sixth-, and eighth-grade* students responded to the prompts. For analysis, a random sample of 6 students was identified from all fourth- and sixth-grade classes: 17 fourth- and 15 sixth-grade classes in the 8 elementary schools. The maximum possible number of fourth-grade students was 102. Due to absence, transfer, and such there were 95 fourth-grade students for whom both fall and spring writing samples were scored. For the sixth grade, the maximum possible number was 90, and, for the foregoing reasons, there were 77 students for whom both fall and spring samples were scored.

Scoring. The scoring system is the basic one developed at the UCLA Center for the Study of Evaluation (Quellmalz and Burry 1983), a version of which is used in the study of writing progress as part of the National Assessment. The scale is generic. That is, it is

---

*Variations in the administration of the stimuli and prompts at eighth grade in the spring led to doubts about the comparability of results within grade and across grades; therefore, the eight-grade fall to spring results are not reported here.

criterial and can be used to analyze the writing of persons of different ages and stages of development. Consequently, it permits the assessment of growth in writing as students progress through the grades. Raters are trained to assess writing from persons of different ages and in different grades according to the same criteria. Three dimensions of writing quality are assessed for each type of writing: focus and organization, support and elaboration of ideas, and grammar and mechanics.

For this study, the raters practiced until the correlation between their ratings was above 0.90, and they repeatedly checked their reliability against a set of writing samples for which scores had been established. Overlapping rating permitted regular checks for reliability. Also, where a rater indicated uncertainty about the correct score, the sample was rated by two other raters. In those cases, if two of the three raters agreed, their score was used. In the cases where all three produced different scores, they were averaged. In the more than 700 samples that were analyzed, averaging was necessary only 10 times.

The results shared in the next two sections focus on the comparison of the distributions of scores obtained from the analysis of the fall and spring expository and persuasive writing samples for grades 4 and 6.

RESULTS: GRADE 4

Grade 4 Expository Writing. Table 3.6 compares the means for the two periods (fall 1992 and spring 1993) for the three dimensions

T A B L E   3.6

MEAN GRADE 4 SCORES ON EXPOSITORY WRITING
FOR FALL 1992 AND SPRING 1993

	Dimensions		
Period	*Focus/Org.*	*Support*	*Grammar/Mech.*
Fall			
Mean	1.6	2.2	2.11
SD	0.55	0.65	0.65
Spring			
Mean	2.8	0.32	3.0
SD	0.94	0.96	0.97

for which quality was assessed (Focus/Organization, Support, and Grammar and Mechanics).

In the fall, the coefficient of correlation between the dimensions of Focus/Organization and Support was 0.56, between the dimensions of Focus/Organization and Grammar/Mechanics was 0.61, and between the dimensions of Support and Grammar/Mechanics was 0.63. In the spring, these were 0.84, 0.65, and 0.74, respectively.

Effect sizes were computed for fall and spring scores: for Focus/ Organization, 2.18; for Support, 1.53; and for Grammar/Mechanics, 1.37.

All these figures are several times the effect-sizes calculated for a year's gain for the national sample and of the baseline gains determined from the 1991-1992 analyses in University Town. For Focus and Organization, the differences are so great that, in the spring, the average student reached the top of the fall distribution, something that does not happen nationally during the entire time from grades 4 to 12.

To illustrate the magnitude of the gain, table 3.7 compares the mean results for the spring fourth-grade assessment to the fall sixth-grade results.

The fourth-grade students ended their year substantially ahead of where the sixth-grade students were at the beginning of the year. They also finished the year with higher scores than where the eighth-grade students began the year on the Focus/Organization (grade 8

T A B L E   3.7

MEAN GRADE 4 SPRING 1993 SCORES ON EXPOSITORY WRITING COMPARED WITH THE MEAN GRADE 6 SCORES FROM FALL 1992

	Dimensions		
	Focus/Org.	*Support*	*Grammar/Mech.*
Grade 4 Spring			
Mean	2.8	3.2	3.0
Grade 6 Fall			
Mean	2.11	2.90	2.87

mean = 2.32) and Support dimensions (grade 8 mean = 2.95) and were close on the Grammar/Mechanics dimension (grade 8 mean = 3.32).

Diagnostic Implications. These findings are particularly interesting to us not only because of their magnitude, but also because expository writing has traditionally been much more difficult to affect through instruction or practice than has narrative writing. Also, the Focus/Organization dimension has been the most difficult dimension to influence within this genre, and competence in the ability to focus and organize a piece of writing has lagged seriously behind the ability to support ideas once selected and the ability to use mechanics to enhance the expression of ideas. As indicated earlier, the concentration of the Models of Teaching/Language Arts Initiative was on literature and writing, with substantial results.

The scale that was used to assess writing quality has six levels, with Level 1 indicating the lowest level of writing quality, and Level 6 the highest level of writing quality. For example, in expository papers rated a Level 1 in the Focus-Organization dimension, it is difficult to identify the subject or the main idea of the writer; in papers rated a Level 6, the subject and the primary message are clear, with key points developed throughout the piece, and the plan or organization is logical.

An examination of the levels of competence students achieved provides information not revealed by gains in scores as such. We estimate that Level 4 on the writing scale is necessary to manage the tasks of secondary education, not just successfully, but to learn *from* writing—to synthesize from multiple sources and to generate new ideas. In fall 1992, just 11 percent of the fourth-grade writing samples were rated at Level 4 or above on one or more dimensions. In spring 1993, 30 percent were rated at Level 4. Once the competence to generate a level of that magnitude has been reached on one or two dimensions, practice and expert instruction should result in a consolidation of all dimensions at that level or higher. However, continuing gains at the rate achieved by these fourth-grade students will be necessary if all the students are to reach the "four" level by the time they enter middle school.

Scores below Level 2 indicate that students are still struggling to express themselves. Once Level 2 is reached, progress becomes easier, provided that there is much practice and expert instruction. The fourth-grade mean in the fall was only 1.6 in the Focus-Organization dimension, indicating that the average student was only in the beginning stages of learning to focus a piece of expository writing.

Only 15 percent of the papers were rated 2.0 or better on the Focus-Organization dimension. In the spring, 15 percent were still rated below 2.0, despite the gains, and the schools had much work to do.

All the schools achieved substantial effects. Between-school variability decreased because some of the schools that traditionally have had somewhat lower achievement than the others gained substantially, reaching the district average or above. The mean gain for the lowest SES school was 1.86, compared to a mean gain of 1.2 for all schools.

Gender as a Factor. As indicated earlier, there are significant gender differences favoring females over males indicated in the results from the National Assessment of Writing Progress. The differences appear by the fourth grade. From then until high school graduation, the mean score for males is around the 30th percentile of the female scores.

In the fall assessment in University Town, the average fourth-grade male was at about the 16th percentile of the female distribution in the Focus and Organization dimension. In the spring assessment, the mean for the males was at about the 33rd percentile of the female distribution. In Support, the male mean was at about the 33rd percentile of the female distribution in both the fall and spring assessments. In the fall assessment, the average fourth-grade male was at about the 20th percentile of the female distribution in the Grammar/Mechanics dimension. In the spring assessment, the male mean was at about the 40th percentile of the female distribution.

University Town serves too few students classified as racial or ethnic "minorities" to make similar analyses meaningful.

Grade 4 Persuasive Writing. The National Assessment of Educational Progress indicated that persuasive writing is in relatively poor shape and that progress across the grades has been minimal. For the University Town fourth grade, the means for the fall samples in persuasive writing were consistent with the national picture. The mean in persuasive writing for Focus and Organization was about 0.2 scale-score points below the score for expository writing, and the mean for Support was about 0.7 scale-score points lower than the mean for Support in expository writing. However, as can be seen in table 3.8, substantial progress was made on both Focus/Organization and Support dimensions during the academic year 1992-93.

In the fall, the coefficient of correlation between the dimensions of Focus/Organization and Support was 0.43, between the dimensions of Focus/Organization and Grammar/Mechanics was 0.31, and between the dimensions of Support and Grammar/Mechanics was

0.55. In the spring, these were 0.51, 0.35, and 0.27, respectively. Anova comparisons of the fall and spring scores were significant for all three dimensions.

Effect-sizes were computed for fall and spring scores: for Focus/ Organization, 0.47; for Support, 1.71; and for Grammar/Mechanics, 0.32.

Although the gains in persuasive writing by the fourth-grade University Town students were much larger than the national gains, the mean in the spring for Focus and Organization was still below 2.0, indicating that the students were still struggling to express themselves with this type of writing. Future efforts to improve the ability to work in the persuasive genre are indicated. By far the largest gains were on the Support dimension: the mean spring scores on the Support dimension are above those with which the sixth grade began the year and are virtually equal to those with which the eighth grade began the year. There were just two dimension scores (out of 285) rated at Level 4. Between the Focus/Organization and Support dimensions, 25 percent were rated at Level 3 in the spring, which means that some students are beginning to spread their wings in the genre.

The achievement by these students and their teachers is considerable, but obviously much more can be achieved in quality of writing.

TABLE 3.8

MEAN GRADE 4 SCORES ON PERSUASIVE WRITING
FOR FALL 1992 AND SPRING 1993

	Focus/Org.	*Support*	*Grammar/Mech.*
		Dimensions	
Fall			
Mean	1.45	1.33	2.31
SD	0.53	0.60	0.73
Spring			
Mean	1.70	2.36	2.54
SD	0.65	0.64	0.73

An important question to explore will be the extent to which the persuasive genre must be taught explicitly.

RESULTS: GRADE 6

Grade 6 Expository Writing. Table 3.9 compares the means for the two periods (fall 1992 and spring 1993) for the three dimensions for which quality was assessed (Focus and Organization, Support, and Grammar and Mechanics).

T A B L E   3.9

MEAN GRADE 6 SCORES ON EXPOSITORY WRITING
FOR FALL 1992 AND SPRING 1993

| | *Dimensions* | | |
	Focus/Org.	*Support*	*Grammar/Mech.*
Fall			
Mean	2.11	2.90	2.87
SD	0.56	0.72	0.67
Spring			
Mean	3.09	3.59	3.41
SD	0.69	0.68	1.00

In the fall, the coefficient of correlation between the dimensions of Focus/Organization and Support was 0.59, between the dimensions of Focus/Organization and Grammar/Mechanics was 0.57, and between the dimensions of Support and Grammar/Mechanics was 0.48. In the spring, these coefficients were 0.70, 0.58, and 0.67, respectively.

Effect sizes were computed for fall and spring scores: for Focus/Organization, 1.75; for Support, 1.10; and for Grammar/Mechanics, 0.81.

All these are several times the effect-sizes for the national sample and for the baseline in University Town. For the dimension of Focus and Organization, the effect size is actually five times the national average and about three and a half times the average for the University Town baseline.

To illustrate the magnitude of the difference, table 3.10 compares the results from the spring 1993 sixth-grade assessment to the results from the fall 1992 eighth-grade assessment.

The sixth-grade students ended their year substantially ahead of where the eighth-grade students were at the beginning of the year.

Again, we pay close attention to how many students reach Level 4 on the writing scale because it indicates the competency to meet the tasks of secondary education. In the fall, 17 percent of the scores on one or another of the dimensions were at Level 4 or above. In the spring, over 50 percent were at Level 4 or above. No scores were below 2.0; only one-sixth of the dimension scores were below 3.0.

As in the case of grade 4, all schools made substantial gains. Between-school variance decreased somewhat because some of the traditionally lower achieving schools narrowed the gap. The success was districtwide.

As in the case of the fourth grade, the differences between males and females narrowed, but differences remained at the end of the year. Gender differences narrowed between fall and spring from nearly 0.4 scale-score points to an average of less than 0.2 scale-score points. If they continued to narrow at that rate for another year, they would disappear entirely.

TABLE 3.10

COMPARISON OF MEANS OF THE SPRING GRADE 6 EXPOSITORY WRITING SCORES WITH THE FALL GRADE 8 WRITING SCORES

	Dimensions		
	Focus/Org.	*Support*	*Grammar/Mech.*
Mean Gd 6 Spring 1993	3.06	3.55	3.57
Mean Gd 8 Fall 1992	2.33	2.95	3.32

Grade 6 Persuasive Writing. Table 3.11 compares the mean scores on persuasive writing on the three dimensions for which writing quality was scored (Focus and Organization, Support, and Grammar and Mechanics) for the fall 1992 and spring 1993 assessments.

In the fall, the coefficient of correlation between the dimensions of Focus/Organization and Support was 0.60, between the dimensions of Focus/Organization and Grammar/Mechanics was 0.65, and between the dimensions of Support and Grammar/Mechanics was 0.48. In the spring, these were 0.64, 0.46, and 0.56, respectively.

Effect sizes were computed for fall and spring scores: for Focus/Organization, -0.13; for Support, 0.47; and for Grammar/Mechanics, 0.53.

The growth in persuasive writing was in the dimensions of Support and of Grammar and Mechanics—about a half scale-score point in each. There was essentially no change in the Focus and Organization dimension. The number of students scoring at Level 3 in focusing and organizing a persuasive piece was basically the same from the fall assessment to the spring assessment (33 to 36), with a few more students scoring at Level 4 in the spring (3 to 9).

TABLE 3.11

MEAN GRADE 6 SCORES ON PERSUASIVE WRITING
FOR FALL 1992 AND SPRING 1993

	Dimensions		
	Focus/Org.	*Support*	*Grammar/Mech.*
Fall			
Mean	2.01	2.11	2.60
SD	0.72	0.81	0.75
Spring			
Mean	1.94	2.49	3.00
SD	0.72	0.71	0.53

The gains in the dimensions of Support and Grammar/Mechanics were substantial, but the ability to focus and organize a message are critical to written communication. Much effort needs to be put into helping students use their persuasive skills in written form. Because of the substantial gains in the dimension of Focus/Organization in the expository genre, there is little doubt that comparable gains can be made in the persuasive area, provided careful instruction is given, but we need to learn the extent to which instruction will have to be genre-specific.

GENDER AS A FACTOR IN WRITING QUALITY

The National Assessment of Educational Progress (Applebee and others 1990; Applebee and others 1994) has consistently reported fairly large gender differences in quality of writing. Generally, the male mean is around the 30th percentile of the female mean, though the proportion of high-scoring males appears to be about the same as the proportion of high-scoring females.

In University Town, the male/female differences in the fall writing samples were similar to the NAEP findings: the male means were about 0.67 SD below the female means (male mean around the 28th percentile of the female mean).

The gap between the quality of writing of males and females narrowed considerably during the year. In the spring writing samples, the males were about 0.40 SD below the female means (male mean around the 37th percentile of the female mean).

We speculate that this gender "equity effect" was a product of the energy generated by all the initiatives and the specific energy generated by the Models of Teaching/Language Arts and Just Read Initiatives.

IMPLEMENTATION AS A FACTOR IN WRITING QUALITY

A cross-schools and cross-teacher analysis revealed substantial differences in the degree of implementation of the Models of Teaching/Language Arts and the Just Read Initiatives. Those differences were reflected in the gains achieved in the quality of writing. An interesting finding was that the degrees of implementation were correlated across the schools, and the mean gain for the highest implementing school in quality of writing was a third greater than the mean gain in the lowest implementing school.

The most dramatic differences in writing quality were between classes in the same schools. Although all teachers implemented the Language Arts Initiative to some degree, differences among some teachers were great enough that although all classes made substantial gains, the mean gains made by the highest implementing teachers were as much as 50 percent higher than those of the lowest implementing teachers.

Differences of this magnitude underscore the equity issues involved in school-renewal efforts: children in some classrooms have significantly greater opportunity to learn and achieve than children in other classrooms.

SUMMARY AND REFLECTIONS ON THE UNIVERSITY TOWN PROGRAM

What did we learn or confirm about student learning and school renewal from studying what happens when teachers are supported for individual, schoolwide, and districtwide initiatives?

WITH RESPECT TO STUDENT LEARNING

Dramatic student gains are possible in a relatively brief time. We have another case where initiatives in curriculum and teaching made rapid and substantial differences in student learning. Of course, this does not mean that *any* change in curriculum or instruction could have such rapid or large effects. In the case of University Town, the curricular structure (inquiry into the reading/writing connection) was well grounded theoretically, and the use of the inductive and concept-attainment models added well-studied, highly successful teaching strategies to the mix.

A key role played by central-office staff in University Town was in keeping the focus of the efforts and actions on student learning. In the midst of a complex social system such as a school district—which is, as in most districts, a population of diverse professionals with many different perceptions, agendas, and needs—keeping this focus was far more difficult than it sounds.

WITH RESPECT TO GOVERNANCE OPTIONS

Clearly all three sources of governance can work: individually governed initiatives, faculty-governed initiatives, and district-governed initiatives all had their place in creating a different level of knowledge-in-practice in University Town. The finding that surprised many was that initiatives generated by all three sources of governance were well accepted. The high degree of approval by teachers of the district initiative runs counter to the current rhetoric that "top-down" initiatives are doomed to fail.

Possibly, this degree of approval resulted from the design of the district initiative, for it was constructed using the central concepts of the "best we know" about school renewal: broad inclusion of personnel in governance; a focus on student learning through instruction and curriculum; breadth of involvement in initiation and study; the provision of time for teachers to work together during the school day every week; a great deal of technical assistance; much sharing of information and use of assessment data; and a great deal of staff development, including the use of the training design and "peer coaching" followup.

The school-based or faculty-based governance initiative, schoolwide action research, was designed using these same concepts. However, the staff development did not include the same degree of practice with the techniques of the action-research process by all members of a faculty as did the districts' Models of Teaching/ Language Arts Initiative. Much of the burden was on each school's facilitation team as they worked to involve all members of the faculty in the critical study process around their collective area of study.

What happened in each school was essentially up to each faculty as a collective unit. If the faculty selected a focus on student learning and anchored their actions in studying student performance in this area and directed their actions at changes in instruction and curriculum, they made substantial progress through action research. When the faculty could not come together on a common student-learning goal or when the process devolved into many special-interest groups, little progress could be found in terms of student learning or cultural change in the school.

The Individually Governed Initiative, IGF, was used primarily for professional development opportunities away from the school or district (75 percent for workshops, conferences, and university courses). While teachers were generally positive about these offsite experiences, they had difficulty relating them to their teaching or to student learning. Speculating a bit, these experiences seemed to function much like a "professional vacation" that provided teachers with an opportunity to explore promising curriculum materials or instructional ideas or management techniques without the pressure or expectation that changes would follow.

WITH RESPECT TO IMPLEMENTATION

There is a relationship between student effects (Just Read, Writing) and the degree of implementation. The relationship relates directly to variance in effects across classrooms and across schools.

Breadth of leadership from teachers, principals, and the district office was essential for implementation and social support in sustaining the districtwide Models of Teaching/Language Arts Initiative and the Schoolwide Action Research Initiative.

Extensive technical assistance was needed both from persons within the schools and the district and from persons external to the schools and the district to support the districtwide Models of Teaching/Language Arts Initiative and the Schoolwide Action Research Initiative.

WITH RESPECT TO CAPABILITY BUILDING, POLITICS, AND THE SOCIAL DIMENSIONS

The University Town Program was designed with capability building at the district and school levels in mind. Much progress was made in enabling personnel to pursue desirable classroom, school, and district changes more effectively. Progress was made in developing the cognitions that support capability building, such as knowledge about how to support individual and organizational changes, and in developing a sense of collective efficacy necessary for organizational renewal.

However, even though many persons in the district have seriously engaged in inquiry into school renewal and though their study and work have moved themselves as educators/scholars far beyond where they began, not enough persons hold the cognitions of inquiry across tasks and domains (instruction, curriculum, staff development, action research) strongly enough to continue to lead the district forward without some external assistance.

The social aspects of conducting schoolwide action research were more problematical than were the technical aspects of collecting and analyzing data. Coming together around a common goal and designing actions directly related to student learning were difficult experiences for most faculties. In retrospect, one year of sustained technical assistance in action research (26 days throughout a 12-month period) and limited technical assistance the second year (8 days) were not enough to enable the district to be capable of sustaining schoolwide action research for school renewal on its own.

A very small percentage of the "faculty of the district"—meaning essentially all teachers and administrators working in the district—were unhappy about working collectively for school renewal, and remained that way, actually feeling "disempowered" by the movement away from how things "were always done." An important "technical assistant role" for external consultants, central-office administrators, building administrators, and facilitators was simply to get people to count how many people were against an initiative, to help people listen to what these individuals were saying and address what could be changed or modified, and to work to prevent a few dissatisfied persons from blocking the collective work of many.

University Town was also a test of the magnitude of change a district can support. Initiatives in governance, teaching, curriculum, assessment, and parent involvement were organized into an approach to school and district renewal. Staff development was continuous, as was the study of implementation of all initiatives. A major political and conceptual challenge was to keep these initiatives integrated and keep other district initiatives at bay, for in various stages of development were initiatives in mathematics, technology, as well as strategic planning. At times district-office personnel, administrators, and teachers felt overwhelmed (and still do), but they have kept going. . . and going. . . and going. . . and have built a learning community in their district that, with all its imperfections, is far stronger and more inquiry oriented and responsive to student learning than when they began their journey.

Now, let's move into our next setting, where a district faculty used action research to build a culture of readers and writers.

READERSVILLE

In Readersville, the purpose was to build a culture of readers. All the teachers, administrators, parents, and children of a district of 11 schools were involved in an "at home" reading program conducted as action research by the entire community. At-home reading of all the students was studied intensively, including effects on quality of writing and on the results from standard tests of reading.

The effects were substantial across the grades. Illustrating with the fifth grade, students came to read an average of 50 books per year, compared to an average of 5 books per year before the effort.

No student read fewer than 15 books. The effects on reading comprehension were substantial, and the success in reading translated to writing, where annual gains in quality more than doubled.

READERSVILLE: BUILDING A CULTURE OF READERS AND WRITERS

BRUCE JOYCE AND JAMES M. WOLF

Can a whole school district engage in action research? Can the staff select an area of focus; collect behavioral data on every student; share those data with every student, teacher, and parent; make an initiative for school improvement; study the effects and modify the initiative; and recycle the process? What are the results in terms of student learning? How do people feel about the process?

We* visit Readersville, a district of 11 schools, and study "Operation Just Read." Just Read is a school-improvement initiative in the language arts. It is designed according to the classic action-research format and is oriented toward increasing the amount of independent, at-home reading by K-12 students. We will trace its origins, design, implementation, and results and reflect on its effects on organizational behavior.

BEGINNING: A CONCERN ABOUT READING

What was to become a complex curriculum initiative began with a series of conversations among teachers, curriculum coordinators,

---

* The first-person plural is used throughout because the authors represent the core action-research team that generated the initiative. The numbers of team members fluctuated throughout; decisions were sometimes made by the 40 persons who were involved throughout, but, when action was taken by any school, its faculty was involved in making the decision. All members of the district therefore participated at some level in the decisions. Members of the core team were involved in all decisions, and others participated in decisions that affected them directly.

building administrators, and the superintendent about how much the kids of Readersville were reading and writing. Typically, the estimates varied enormously. Some folks thought that the students read a great deal; others thought that they read a little or not at all. Similarly, estimates of writing ranged from frequently ("After all, we use the 'whole language' approach.") to "a little journal-writing and that's about all, thank you." Discussions about variance in reading and writing activity were only a step above chaotic because of the different frames of reference the members of the group brought to the problem. Altogether, a sequence of discussions involved about 40 people: the 8 curriculum coordinators, 11 principals, and about 20 teachers, approximately one-fifth of the district's professional personnel.

The curriculum coordinators became a little upset that we didn't really have a good base of information, especially because the district had stressed the importance of wide independent reading and extensive writing. So, a decision was made to collect some systematic data in one elementary school and one high school.

FROM CONCERN TO STUDY: COLLECTING BASELINE DATA

In each elementary classroom a file was set up in which the children recorded their independent reading and stored their writing. A similar procedure was followed in the high school English classes. For the little ones, parents kept records of what their children read each evening. For 14 weeks the data were collected.

We selected a random sample of students who were studied in greater depth, for we had a number of questions about how accurate the self-reports were. The study convinced us that the records were reflective of the reading the students had done. The self-report records consistently underestimated the reading done, but just slightly. Fears by some teachers that the students would exaggerate the number of books read turned out to have no basis in fact. Periodic studies over the next two years confirmed the general accuracy of the self-reports.

ORGANIZING THE BASELINE DATA

The data were organized to display trends for each student, classroom, and the school for each week. Thus, trends could be seen at all three levels. For example, table 4.1 shows what the data looked

TABLE 4.1

A FIFTH-GRADE CLASS: NUMBER OF BOOKS READ BY
FIVE STUDENTS DURING ONE WEEK

Student	Number of Books Recorded
1	1
2	2
3	0
4	0
5	0

TABLE 4.2

A FIFTH-GRADE CLASS:
NUMBER OF BOOKS RECORDED BY FIVE STUDENTS
OVER FOUR WEEKS

Student	Number of Books Recorded			
	Week One	Week Two	Week Three	Week Four
1	1	1	0	1
2	2	0	1	0
3	0	1	0	1
4	0	0	2	0
5	0	0	0	0

like for five students in one fifth-grade class at the end of a particular week.

It is easy to see that three of the students recorded no books read; one student read one book; and one student read two books. Table 4.2 shows what the picture was like for those five students over a four-week period.

From this type of table, totals and averages could be computed for each week for each student, class, and school. Gradually the picture emerged as data on the amounts of reading accumulated over time.

TABLE 4.3

MEAN NUMBER OF BOOKS READ PER STUDENT
DURING 14-WEEK BASELINE PERIOD
BY GRADE

Grade	Mean Number of Books
One	21
Two	35
Three	10
Four	4
Five	3
Six	3

BOOKS READ

The baseline survey was completed 14 weeks into the school year, on November 6, 1989. In the elementary school, our worst fears were confirmed (see table 4.3).

INTERPRETING THE DATA

First, in the primary grades, where most of the reading was of picture-story books, we found that about one-third of the students were engaged in very little reading outside of the reading instruction periods, though most of them had the skills to handle simply written books. Many of the grade 1 and 2 students read about one hour per week at home, enough for about two titles a week, which did not seem like a lot to us.

We watched grades 3 to 6 closely, where we would hope a habit of reading would become firmly established, but where studies have actually shown that a slump is more typical (see Chall 1983). In grade 3, one-third of the students accounted for 60 percent of the books read. Several students had done virtually no independent reading.

The grade 4 students averaged only four books for the period. The high was six books. Several students had recorded no titles. The grade 5 students averaged less than three books for the 14-week period. The high was five (about a book every three weeks). The grade 6 students also averaged less than three books, and the high was five. In both grades, many students recorded no books read.

The picture was worse in a second elementary school that joined the baseline study voluntarily. Twenty-seven percent of the students in this school did not read a book during the 14-week period. For those who did read at least one book, the average for grade 6 was 2.5; for grade 5, 4.6; and for grade 3, 7.0. Half of the grade 2 students did no independent reading.

We interpreted our data to mean that many of our youngest readers become somewhat connected to the world of the picture-story book during the first two years of schooling, but that few of them are penetrating that literature extensively. During grades 3 and 6, the next level of literature should be consumed by our students, but if our survey is anywhere near the mark, it appears that was not happening. If the 14-week period is representative of the four years between grades 3 and 6, then the average student would read only about 50 books during the entire 4 years when they were in grades 3 to 6. The highest consumers would read about 75. That is such a small sample of the books in our libraries that the body of literature as such would be virtually unknown to them. For the students who have virtually stopped reading outside of textbooks, the picture was abysmal.

The profile of the high school independent reading was worse yet. Forty-eight percent of the students read no books at all during the baseline period. The other students averaged fewer than two books during the period. Only 5 percent read as much as a book every two weeks.

The implications for learning to write are as considerable as they are for reading. The connection of literature to writing—the use of books read as models for the personal writing process—can by no stretch of the imagination occur at the levels of reading that we discovered. We followed Heller (1991) in speculating that increasing the amounts of literature read is a key to the improvement of the writing process. Instruction that can capitalize on many models of writing and on models made available through wide reading is likely to be much more effective than instruction in the absence of these models.

ADDING TEST DATA TO OUR FILE: COMPETENCE AND READING HABITS

The case-study students were also administered, at the beginning of the baseline period, the Reading Power Test and California Tests of Basic Skills (CTBS) battery in reading and language. The results of these assessments led us to ask whether amounts of reading were a function of competence in reading as measured by those tests. The answer is "no." For example, our sample of sixth-grade students were all above the 80th percentile for their grade on the power test, with independent reading levels of 5.0 or better.

From the standpoint of their ability to read, virtually all the elementary school library was available to them. They just weren't using it. Although there was, of course, variance in reading competence, all the students in the sample at every grade level were competent enough that they could read substantial numbers of the books that were available to them in the school and public libraries.

The CTBS scores were generally in line with those of the Power Test. The distribution was normal; the means somewhat above the national average; and the range from the low teens to the 99th percentile. We had to face the fact that we had students in the very top of the national distribution who did not appear to have a well-developed habit of reading. The coefficient of correlation between number of books reported and CTBS scores was just 0.15.

The standard test scores of the high school students displayed a mean (the 55th percentile on the total reading and total language batteries) similar to that of the elementary students. The range was comparable as well, with more high-scoring students and somewhat fewer low-scoring students than the national average.

Put another way, the levels of competence and achievement of our students, judged by the tests, looked pretty good when compared with the nation as a whole. We simply shared what appears to be a national problem—most of the students *can* read, but many do not exercise their competence much outside of required reading in school subjects.

MAKING THE INITIATIVE

We decided to engineer an initiative in the elementary school that had participated in the baseline study, examine its results, and see if we could devise an approach that could be used in all the elementary schools. The objective was to increase the amounts of independent reading markedly by mounting a campaign that would include the extensive involvement of parents.

The strategy included three components:

First, the collection of data continued. Data were used throughout to help students, classes, and schools measure progress and hold celebrations of success. The data were organized on a weekly basis so that building leadership teams and study teams of teachers could reflect on them, classes and teams of students could see their progress, and individuals could see how much they were reading and writing and what they were reading and writing. In addition, teachers used the data to study *what* as well as *how much* the students were reading as a basis for offering guidance and encouragement. (Classroom libraries were augmented so that teachers could easily guide their students in book selection.)

Second, the project was started with an aggressive campaign to encourage parents and students to increase amounts of at-home reading. Meetings were held to signal the beginning of the campaign. Newsletters, including samples of books read and writing produced by the children, were distributed. Paper chains, containing titles of books read, hung from ceilings and doors. Pizza parties, "T-shirt" parties, complete with "Just Read" logos and the like, were employed. The physical environment of the school was draped with writing, notes on books, and computer-generated advertisements for books. Parents were given ideas for reading projects, book clubs, trading fairs, and writing-at-home projects.

Third, individual, classroom, and school goals were set. Ways of displaying progress were devised, from charts to chains of animals representing books read. Ways of celebrating progress were generated for individuals, classes, and schools. These included certificates, notes sent home, announcements in newsletters, celebratory parties, and a host of other devices.

THE EFFECTS ON THE QUANTITY OF READING

Our first question, as we examined the folders and counted the number of books read and compositions created, was to estimate whether Operation Just Read increased the quantity of reading and writing.

The 14-week period after the program kickoff (the first target period) was compared to the 14-week baseline to generate our first estimate of impact. The data are displayed in table 4.4.

The increases in the primary grades were gratifying, though the lack of increase in grade 3 was puzzling. In subsequent years grade 3 increased as much as did the others—this pilot was the only time that a third grade didn't respond to the initiative with substantial increases in amounts of at-home reading.

The increases in grades 4, 5, and 6 are what we hoped to see as a first level of impact, though we were not satisfied. That the average fifth- and sixth-grade student increased to about a book each week is

T A B L E   4.4

BOOKS READ BY GRADE AND PERIOD
COMPARISON OF BASELINE AND FIRST TARGET PERIOD

	Baseline		First Target	
	Mean	Range	Mean	Range
Grade 1	21	0-28	47	7-89

(Only one child read fewer than 28 books during the first target period.)

	Mean	Range	Mean	Range
Grade 2	35	2-71	50	8-104

(Only one child read fewer than one book per week during the first target period.)

Grade 3	10	3-24	11	1-23

(The number of books stayed about the same, but the complexity and length increased.)

Grade 4	4	1-5	8	3-29

(The mean doubled.)

Grade 5	3	1-5	16	4-38

(The mean increased by five times. The lowest number was higher than the previous mean.)

Grade 6	3	1-5	18	6-38

(The mean increased six times. The lowest number doubled the previous mean.)

a productive increase from one book in five weeks. But half the students were reading less than a book each week, so we decided we had some distance to go before we would be satisfied. Overall, it appeared that the uppergrade students were reading from three to six times the number of books that they were reading during the baseline period.

We were encouraged enough to continue the initiative and expand it to include all nine elementary schools in the district.

THE SECONDARY SCHOOL: READING

The average number of books read increased to one every two-and-a-half weeks (from one every seven weeks). The number of nonindependent readers was reduced to zero, with no student reading fewer than two books during the first target period. Book-a-week regulars began to appear (no fewer than two per class). All students now knew that no one was avoiding the independent reading of books. Reading was not quite the height of fashion, but it was no longer in the category of deviant behavior.

Important for our future planning, we discovered that individual differences among teachers affected the influence of the initiative. Classes of some teachers increased reading as little as 50 percent, while in other classrooms the amount of reading by students increased four to seven times over the baseline. We speculated that a concerted "all school" effort would gradually reduce the "teacher effect" as regular reading became an ingrained habit across the secondary school.

ADDING STANDARD TEST RESULTS TO THE PICTURE

Our objective was to induce students, with the aid of their parents and cheerleading and counsel from their teachers, to increase their reading. We wanted to build a culture of readers (and, not incidentally, writers). "Raising test scores" was not an objective. However, in the pilot elementary school, a study of standard test scores for the fifth grade indicated that the difference between student performance in the fall and spring administrations of the CTBS battery was substantial. The elementary student mean had increased from the 48th national percentile to the 66th. In the high school, the fall mean was at the 54th percentile, and the spring mean was the 58th percentile.

Writing samples from the case-study students were submitted to analytic scoring using an instrument developed by the UCLA Center for the Study of Evaluation. Comparisons were made between the writing during the baseline period and the first target period. For the elementary students, the average gain was about two-and-a-half times the national average gain made in a school year. The gains cannot be attributed with certainty to Just Read and Write, but we were curious enough to accompany the next year's effort, which included all the elementary schools, with a thoroughgoing examination. We sought to determine not only the quantities of reading and writing generated by the initiative, but also whether there were systematic effects on standard test performance or on quality of writing. The fifth grade was chosen for the intensive testing program, though all grades were involved in the second year of Operation Just Read.

THE SECOND YEAR

The building leadership teams of the elementary schools oriented their faculties. Data collection was introduced at the beginning of the year and followed, at the end of the first quarter, by the launching of the campaign and the development of the celebrations generated by each faculty. Data were organized and used as before, creating a formative-evaluation process that operated at the level of the student, the classroom, the faculty study group (clusters of teachers), the school, and the district.

In addition, the California Tests of Basic Skills (CTBS) reading and language battery was administered to all fifth-grade students in September and March. Three standard writing stimuli were used to elicit examples of expository, descriptive, and persuasive writing in September, January, and just before the end of the school year. The fifth-grade classes were compared in terms of amounts of reading and writing generated and the results of the testing program in reading and writing.

AMOUNTS OF READING GENERATED

For the entire year, including the first quarter, the mean number of books recorded are shown in table 4.5 for the grade 2 to 6 children who were in school for the entire year. In each grade there were about 300 children for whom we had complete records for the full year. Altogether, the records of 1,553 children were included in the analysis.

The average student from grades 4 to 6 recorded 50 titles, or about one and three-quarters per week. This number is at least 10

T A B L E   4.5

MEAN NUMBER OF BOOKS
RECORDED FOR THE YEAR BY GRADE

Grade	Mean Number of Books Recorded
2	102
3	82
4	55
5	45
6	51

T A B L E   4.6

FIFTH-GRADE TITLES RECORDED BY QUARTER:
MEANS FOR THE ENTIRE POPULATION

	Quarter			
	First	*Second*	*Third*	*Fourth*
Mean	4.6	12.5	13.75	14.3

times the national average, as near as we can tell from the various ways of estimating it. Grade 2 students read about twice as many titles, but, of course, they were shorter and less complex books. Grade 3 was in transition to longer books, which is reflected in the figures. We were pleased that grade 3 responded as well to the initiative as did the other grades.

The trend was sharply upward from the first quarter to the second, and then continued gradually upward. The fifth-grade trend is shown in table 4.6.

Nonreading was greatly reduced. During the first quarter, 11.4 percent of the fifth-grade students recorded no titles. This was reduced to 3 percent in the fourth quarter. During the data-collection-only period (the first quarter), 16 percent of the males recorded no titles, dropping to 2.1 percent by the last quarter. Twenty-two students read fewer than 10 books during the year. Only six children read fewer than five books. A quarter of the students averaged over two books per week during the year. The evidence appears clear to us that Operation Just Read had an enormous impact on the amounts of out-of-school reading done by the students. Yet it is, from a technical standpoint, a very easy initiative to implement.

The implementation was uneven, however. Schools differed in the amounts of reading generated, as did classrooms within schools, despite the schoolwide character of the effort and the continuous flow of information to teachers, students, and parents.

DIFFERENCES AMONG SCHOOLS: THE FIFTH-GRADE CLASSES

The fifth-grade classes illustrate dramatically the differences in implementation (table 4.7).

T A B L E 4.7	

MEAN NUMBER OF BOOKS READ BY THE FIFTH-GRADE STUDENTS IN THE NINE SCHOOLS DURING THE ACADEMIC YEAR

School	Mean Number of Books Read
1	64
2	62
3	55
4	52
5	43
6	38
7	30
8	28
9	27

Implementation was judged by the amounts of reading, in number of books, reported by the students during the 1990-91 school year. In the four highest schools, the average number of books reported was 56.5, with a range of 52 to 64. In the three lowest, the average number of books read was 28.3, with a range of 27 to 30. Thus, the average student in the highest implementing schools read just about twice as many books as did the average student in the lower implementing schools.

It is worth noting that the lowest implementing schools had succeeded in raising the number of books reported to about four times what it was before the initiative began, which is no small achievement. However, the effect was twice as great in the four highest implementation settings, with the average fifth-grade student now reading about 1.8 books per week during the school year.

Those schools that generated the most titles read in the fifth grade also generated more writing. The three lowest implementation schools, in terms of books read, were also the three lowest in terms of the production of items of expressive writing.

EFFECTS ON QUALITY OF WRITING

Operation Just Read and Write was designed to increase writing as well as reading and did so. As indicated earlier, the higher implementation schools in reading (those that generated the larger number of titles read) also generated the larger number of writing samples recorded. The analysis here will be confined to a comparison of the higher and lower implementation schools.

In September and again in June, standard writing stimuli designed to elicit descriptive, expository, and persuasive writing were administered to all the fifth-grade students and scored using the holistic analysis procedures developed at the UCLA Center for the Study of Evaluation. The important products of the analysis are scores (on a six-point scale) that depict the clarity of focus of the writing (the establishment of clear themes and arguments) and the use of supporting detail to elaborate those themes and arguments.

Table 4.8 presents a comparison of high- and low-implementation schools.

For high-implementation schools, the difference between the fall and spring samples show an effect size of 3.4, compared with a national average gain of 0.10 (Applebee and others 1990 [1988 NAEP Writing Assessment]).

For low-implementation schools, the difference between the fall and spring scores amounts to an effect size of 1.2, compared to the national effect size of 0.16.

HIGH- AND LOW-QUANTITY READERS IN HIGH- AND LOW-IMPLEMENTATION SCHOOLS

There were substantial differences in the amounts of reading done by the students in all the schools. In this analysis, the three highest quantity readers and three lowest quantity readers in each

TABLE 4.8		
PRETEST AND POSTTEST COMPARISONS OF HIGH- AND LOW-IMPLEMENTATION SCHOOLS ON QUALITY OF WRITING ANALYSES		
	High Implementation	*Low Implementation*
Pretest		
Mean	2.73	2.65
Posttest		
Mean	3.33	2.95
Mean Gain	.60	.30

school were identified and compared in a further effort to search for information about how different amounts of reading affect skill development. We wanted a picture of what we needed to do to affect student growth substantially, aside from the obvious informational and attitudinal benefits of increased amounts of reading and writing.

Table 4.9 compares the highest and lowest quantity readers in the highest and lowest implementation schools in terms of amounts of reading and writing done and their pretest and posttest scores on the quality of writing analyses.

In terms of quantity of reading, the average student in the lowest implementation schools read six times more titles during the year than the baseline estimates (which appear to be about at the national average: 5). The average *lowest quantity* readers in the *lowest implementation schools* read three times more than the baseline. The lowest quantity readers in the highest implementation schools read more than five times the baseline. In the lowest implementation schools, the highest quantity readers read 14 times the baseline, and the highest quantity readers in the highest implementation schools read 20 times more than the baseline.

Initial CTBS Scores. Comparing the highest and lowest quantity readers in the highest and lowest implementation schools results in an interesting finding. In the high-implementation schools, the mean for the high-quantity readers was NCE (normal-curve equivalent) 57 and for the low-quantity readers, NCE 52. In the lowest implementation schools, the difference between the high- and low-quantity readers was NCE 13 (67-54). Thus, although there was no correlation between initial CTBS scores in reading and amounts read for the population as a whole, in the lower implementation schools the high-quantity readers did appear to have higher scores. The higher implementation schools drew more of the readers who began with average and below-average scores into the most extensive reading habits, possibly because the higher amounts of energy overcame the usual effects of initial reading ability.

Comparisons of Pre- and Post-CTBS Scores. In the highest implementation schools, both high- and low-quantity readers gained significantly in normal-curve-equivalent percentile ranks for the reading battery (mean NCE gain 8 and 6, respectively). In the high-implementation schools, the mean pretest and posttest percentile ranks were about the same for both high- and low-quantity readers as they were in the lowest implementation schools.

The total language NCE mean percentiles were also about the same for pre- and post-administrations for high- and low-quantity readers in all the schools.

| **T   A   B   L   E   4.9** | | | | | | | |

HIGH- AND LOW-QUANTITY READERS AND WRITERS IN HIGH- AND LOW-IMPLEMENTATION SCHOOLS: CTBS DATA AND QUALITY OF WRITING							
		Reading CTBS		*Writing Quality*		*Quantity*	
Schools	*Readers*	*Fall*	*Spr*	*Fall*	*Spr*	*Rdg*	*Wrtg*
Highest Level (2)	High Qty.(12)	55	63	2.8	3.6	114	76
	Low Qty. (8)	55	61	2.6	3.3	24	82
High Level (2)	High Qty. (16)	54	57	2.8	3.4	93	71
	Low Qty. (13)	52	52	2.7	3.0	29	49
Lowest Level (3)	High Qty.(15)	67	65	2.7	3.1	73	60
	Low Qty.(17)	54	52	2.6	2.8	15	33

Quality of Writing: Comparison of Pretest and Posttest Scores. Initial mean scores were similar for both categories of students in all three levels of schools. However, the mean gains in the highest implementation schools were 0.8 points for the high-quantity readers and 0.7 points for the low-quantity readers. The high-quantity readers in the high-implementation schools gained an average of 0.6; the low-quantity readers, 0.3. Somewhat smaller, but significant, gains were made by both categories of students in the low-implementation schools.

The highest readers in the low-implementation schools read nearly as much as did the highest readers in the high-implementation schools. However, the highest readers in the high-implementation schools gained much more in quality of writing (ES 1.44) than did the highest readers in the low-implementation schools.

The lowest readers in the high-implementation schools outgained the highest readers in the low-implementation schools with respect to quality of writing (ES 0.26).

For high and low readers in the low-implementation schools, there were virtually no differences in gains in quality of writing, though the number of books read was quite different.

What we have here is a real "cohort" effect. The more energetic schools pulled all the students along, whereas in the low-implementation schools students who read more made little improvement in the quality of their writing.

THE CTBS BATTERY ON READING

Giving the battery to the fifth-grade students in September (hereafter referred to as the pretest) and again in March (the posttest), 21 weeks after the first administration, enabled us to compare the results. The tests are reported in national percentile ranks, normal curve equivalents, grade-level equivalents (GLE), and standard scores. Each has its uses.

The question in this analysis is whether the effects of the different levels of implementation of Just Read and Write are reflected in gains on the CTBS battery. Before comparing the four highest implementation schools with the three lowest implementation schools, let us examine the scores of the district fifth-grade students as a whole, as they are presented in table 4.10.

The normal-curve-equivalent gain speaks for itself. With respect to the GLE, the prediction from the pretest is that the mean gain at 21 weeks would be .57. There was an excess gain of .53. Roughly speaking, the average was where it would have been expected to be 40 months after the pretest; the gain was about twice what would have been expected had there been no treatment. With respect to the Scale Scores, the difference between the district and the national average gain was significant at the .001 level (F=21.61). Using the national average as a control, the effect size was .44.

Table 4.11 presents the mean pretest and posttest results for the high- and low-implementation schools on the comprehension test of the reading battery.

The analysis compared the gains made by the students in the high- and low-implementation schools, covarying for prior learning history as described above. In other words, the question is how much the students gained *above* or below the amounts predicted by their prior history. In table 4.11, we can see that the difference against prediction based on the GLE was very large indeed.

T A B L E   4.10

PRE- AND POST-TEST RESULTS ON THE CTBS READING
COMPREHENSION TEST IN STANDARD SCORES, NORMAL
CURVE EQUIVALENTS, AND GRADE-LEVEL EQUIVALENTS

	Mean GLE	Mean NCE	Mean Scale Score
Pretest	5.7	54.5	717
SD	2.6	48.5	
Posttest	6.8	58.1	736
SD	2.8	2.7	
Gain	1.1	3.6	19

T A B L E   4.11

COMPARISON OF THE HIGH- AND LOW-
IMPLEMENTATION SCHOOLS ON THE CTBS
COMPREHENSION TEST

	High-Implementation Schools	Low-Implementation Schools
NCE		
Mean PRE	51.7	55.2
Mean POST	55.3	56.3
GLE		
Mean PRE	5.5	5.9
Mean POST	6.85	6.2
Mean GAIN	1.35	0.3
Predicted Gain	0.52	0.61
Gain Over Pred	0.83	0.31

THE THIRD YEAR AND BEYOND

The next year, the low-implementation schools profited from the
experience, and all the schools reached the level the high-implementation schools had reached during the second year. Some schools
exceeded those levels. Nonreading was virtually eliminated. Gender
and ethnic differences in quality of writing diminished greatly. The

initiative on writing was expanded, and the faculties began to study quality of writing and how to improve it through instruction.

APPLICATIONS IN OTHER SETTINGS

Just Read is a curriculum-augmentation initiative that involves the community. Implementation required substantial "nurturant" staff development to help teachers, students, and parents learn to collect data on reading and celebrate accomplishments. The program has been disseminated to a number of other school districts whose data are currently available to us.

As in Readersville, building a community of readers has been the primary goal in these other settings as well, which means, among other things, reducing or eliminating the phenomenon of "not reading" independently at home. In fall 1993, three schools in the Newport/Costa Mesa Unified School District in California collected their baseline data and then began their community-involvement projects. These schools were particularly interesting because, for several years, they had been using some of the more conventional programs to increase reading both in and out of school. However, Just Read brought the data-based action-research format to them.

One school, in a community where many of the children were just learning English, moved from a baseline of an average of only 1 book per child per month to over 11 books per child per month.

A second school, in a neighborhood of affluent families, discovered that more than half of their students were not reading at home at all! By March, that number had been reduced to 15 percent as the school doubled the number of books read per week. By May, all the children were reading. Altogether, the 500 children read 70,000 books that year.

A third school, also in an affluent neighborhood, tripled the at-home reading in the first four months and nearly eliminated nonreading at home. Both teachers and parents learned that goals could be much higher than they had been satisfied with before in the amounts of reading done by the average student and in the number of children who could be reached.

In University Town, the average student in the district's elementary schools now reads about 100 books a year, independent of assigned reading. Perhaps as important, the kindergarten students now share about 150 books per year in the "read-to'" or "read-with" mode. As described in chapter 3, the initiative is combined with an intensive effort focused on the study of teaching and the reading-writing connection, with large effects on the quality of writing and substantial rises on the vocabulary and comprehension subtests of the Iowa Tests of Basic Skills.

In Inner City (chapter 5), at the kindergarten level, parents of K-12 students in a "project school" have been reading an average of a book a day to or with their children or listening to their children's reading daily. The result is that those children are virtually indistinguishable, in standard-test terms in reading or mathematics, from suburban children.

In Glynn County, Georgia, under the leadership of Pamela Lewis, the assistant superintendent for instruction, the nine elementary schools and three middle schools embarked on the Just Read program in fall 1994. They are moving along in their first year of struggle, but already one of the middle schools has reduced the number of "non-readers" from about 350 to about 50, showing how rapidly positive changes of magnitude can be made.

Other schools and districts are making similar progress. It appears that Just Read travels well.

THE SOCIAL-PSYCHOLOGICAL DIMENSION

In Readersville and in the other settings where Just Read is operating, the reactions of administrators, parents, and teachers have been fascinating. Although Just Read has settled into a comfortable routine in each setting, there has been considerable initial turmoil. A multiple-role leadership team needs to exert considerable energy at the beginning of each school year, or many teachers would drop the program. Several aspects of the project seem to draw an initial negative reaction on the part of some teachers and administrators:

1. The confrontation with the baseline data has generated controversy in each setting. Part of the controversy arises from the belief that the self-report data on reading will be inaccurate because students will lie about their reading. In each setting, case studies of students have indicated that the data are accurate or a slight underestimate of the actual numbers of books read, but many teachers remain unconvinced until the data-collection has been established for several months. Even then, a few will raise the issue and persist in their belief that student reports are unreliable.

In middle-class settings, there is initial disbelief and discouragement by many as the initial data reveal that so many students read little or not at all. Some folks want to kill the messenger.

In all settings, there is great variance in reaction to those data in terms of whether the situation can change. Some teachers become immediately determined to make a difference, and some depict the picture as hopeless. Some who have already been promoting reading become angry as the data reveal the low levels of reading that are going on.

Even where the faculties vote overwhelmingly to participate, a certain number of teachers create a substantial uproar over the burden of data collection (about 5 to 10 minutes per week, largely by the children). The complaints about the burden never totally cease, even when success is achieved. There are continual efforts to get rid of the development of the weekly, formative picture.

2. During planning, there is extensive discussion about parents and rewards. In every setting, about half the teachers voice the opinion that the parents are not interested in the education of their children, that television and recreational activities leave no time for reading, and that the program will fail unless it is converted to "sustained silent reading." Many believe that celebration will not have any effect and that grades and other "rewards" are necessary. Some believe that the titles should be tightly controlled; if not, the students will read "junk." Others state that reading magazines and newspapers is just as worthwhile as reading books. When the program begins, only very cheerful and active leadership by affirmative teachers and principals keeps things going.

3. As the publicity begins, there is an immediate increase in amounts of reading and a very positive reaction by most parents and community members, though a small number object to the initiative, usually on the grounds that *their* kids don't have time to read and will not "look as good" as the average student. A few want tangible rewards, because that is how they get their kids to do things. The majority are very pleased and appreciate the collaboration of the school in something they have wanted for a long time but have not known, in most cases, how to achieve—to have children who not only *can* read, but *do* read.

4. Within a month or so, many teachers report that the increases in reading have positive side effects on the efficacy of language-arts instruction, that discussions are more lively and informed, and that many children are surprised and pleased at how pleasurable and informative reading is. However, implementation is uneven across teachers and schools. Some teachers hope to "wait it out" despite the good feelings and successes of their neighbors. Gradually, most of

them are drawn in, but some continue to resist and complain throughout the year.

5. After a couple of months, it becomes apparent that the program is a success for all but about 10 percent of the students. The leadership struggles with this, but individualized efforts with parents and children reduce the number of nonreaders to zero. To succeed, the leadership group has to overcome the belief by many that "you just can't reach everybody" and the willingness to write off a small number as unreachable.

6. When the second year begins, the leadership teams find, to their surprise, that the process has not become institutionalized. Although it is easier to reinstitute the program than it was to start it, the negative teachers attack again, raising the questions about time, unreliability of records, and futility until reinitiation is accomplished.

SUMMARY: EQUITY AND EFFICACY

One of the clear findings from the studies of Just Read is the very large variance in initial implementation among schools and among classrooms in the same school. Because the demographic factors that so often account for variance in implementation appear to be overcome by the program, we need to turn to other explanations. Our current theory is that the explanation resides in the sense of efficacy felt by faculties as communities and by teachers as individuals. Do they explain variance in achievement as due to the quality of curriculum and instruction or do they ascribe it to the characteristics of the students and the community?

Put simply, we believe that the faculties that think they can affect student achievement through their own efforts succeed in involving the community and developing the symbiotic relationship necessary to make Just Read work without great struggle. Within those faculties, the teachers who believe they can succeed regardless of external factors bring their students along into the world of reading.

We are completely puzzled by the number of teachers who do not agree with the premise of the program that the curriculum in reading and writing does not end with the development of skill, but needs to ensure that the children practice those skills in the course of educating themselves through independent reading and writing.

Now, let's visit a complex school-improvement program in one of America's most depressed and divided cities.

INNER CITY

The Inner City Initiative for School Improvement was designed to provide excellence in student learning and in the workplace of educational professionals.

With respect to the students, the intent was to ensure that no student be disadvantaged educationally, regardless of conditions in the home, to ensure normal or above-average growth in personal qualities, social skills, values, citizenship, and academic work.

With respect to teachers and administrators, the intent was to build a self-renewing organization where innovative collegiality and the study of teaching and curriculum are the norm. Five "demonstration schools," whose faculties had voted to participate, were studied intensively as they implemented several complex initiatives.

Despite voting to work collectively to change the school and improve student learning, many teachers, and nearly all central-office personnel, found it difficult to work together. In fact, various segments of the teachers and administrators resisted specific elements of the program after giving nominal assent to them

Although implementation was uneven, several components developed quite well and very rapidly, and student learning was substantially affected in some areas. The success did not reduce the organizational chaos. Although many teachers became much more optimistic about the capabilities of the children, few were willing to reduce their combativeness within the organization in order to build collaborative modes of working.

CHAPTER 5

THE INNER CITY PROGRAM: A VOYAGE WITH STAFF DEVELOPMENT

BRUCE JOYCE, BEVERLY SHOWERS, AND HENRY IZUMIZAKI

Can the desperately needy schools of our inner cities respond productively to a complex of powerful initiatives designed to improve the education of their students *immediately?*

The Inner City Initiative for School Improvement was designed to provide excellence in student learning and in the workplace of educational professionals. With respect to the students, the intent was to ensure that no student be disadvantaged educationally, regardless of conditions in the home. For each student, the initiative sought to ensure normal or above-average growth in personal qualities, social skills, values, citizenship, and academic work. With respect to teachers and administrators, the intent was to build a self-renewing organization where innovative collegiality and the study of teaching and curriculum are the norm.

Inner cities are not unique in the problems they have in making productive changes in curriculum and instruction, but the acute needs of city schools and the failure of massive efforts to improve them combine to dramatize their problems. When the project began, the situation in Inner City epitomized the problem of all our cities in making the massively funded Title I, special education, bilingual, and other well-intentioned federal and state efforts work to give their children a good start in life. In 40 of the district's 100 schools, *all* of the children were served by several of these programs beginning in grade 1. By grade 12, only a handful had exited from the "special" programs into the "regular" school program.

As in other problem-riddled, inner-city school districts, the failure to make the major categorical programs work dramatizes the problem of developing the capacity to change. Administrators, school faculties, and community members simply have not been able to make the changes in curriculum and instruction that will get the job done. *Worse, they have had 30 years of experience trying to improve things, and their frustration continues to grow.*

The problems of the inner cities were well documented by the late 1950s (see Passow, ed., 1963; Conant 1961). The large-scale categorical programs were developed in the early 1960s to ameliorate these conditions. Yet, "death at an early age" (Kozol 1967) continues. Blame is often assigned to federal and state regulators, central administrators, principals, and, of course, teachers. Frequently, they blame each other. Yet the continued "practice of failure" belies any pointing of fingers. All categories of personnel are stymied equally. All feel disempowered by decades of doing what has not worked. Whole careers have been spent as Title I teachers, administrators, and curriculum developers without figuring out what to do that will work better.

In this chapter we focus on the social and the technical aspects of change in equal measure as we reflect on a project designed to improve student learning and build a collaborative workplace in five of the lowest achieving schools in a chaotic inner city. The project developers intended to use the experiences in those schools to lead the way in changing how the district does business: to change the organization of the central office, the involvement of parents, and the relationship between teachers and administrators at all levels. The direction of change was toward greater self-renewing capability in the district.

As we concentrate on the efforts made in Inner City, we want to make clear that we are not promoting the initiatives we describe or pretending that educators in other equally unlikely settings are not doing good things. Rather, some of the recent efforts in several other urban settings speak, as does the one we describe, to the feasibility of making substantial changes, and making them quickly, in the educational environments that are available for students in the inner city.

THE LARGER CONTEXT

That America's inner-city schools possess serious problems is not a closely guarded secret. Because the city schools have not improved palpably despite a generation of costly efforts to improve them, pessimism and skepticism about the prospect of reform efforts increase. Some scholars are flatly melancholy about the prospects (Sarason 1982, 1990; Cuban 1990). Families who acquire the means tend to flee the city center, despite its importance to their cultural and economic life. Ethnic groups battle for resources and attention, fearful that "their people" are being shortchanged. Even though city budgets for education are already substantially lower per pupil than in rural and suburban districts, state and federal lawmakers and executives, discouraged by the progress being made, cut well-intentioned programs, further placing at a disadvantage the urban centers that so badly need their resources to stem disintegration, cope with the unrest of their populations, and begin the climb back to a higher quality of life.

Citizens and teachers struggle to find ways out of the morass. Proposals such as the "voucher," which would bankrupt the large city systems, manifest the hopelessness with which many citizens regard the system. Teachers respond variably to the problems of the urban schools. Some dig in proudly and take on the attitude of front-line soldiers in a dangerous war that threatens their nation. Some become despondent. Perhaps most serious of all, recruitment of fresh educational troops for the cities is a virtual nightmare and will remain so unless messages of success can be broadcast from our most difficult educational settings.

In this environment of failure, teachers, administrators, and parents are often separated from and even antagonistic toward one another. There is much blaming and pointing of fingers. Low expectations for the students are endemic on all sides, which compounds the problem of generating reform—it's hard to be optimistic when you don't have confidence that the students have potential.

Because of the degree to which large-scale urban school reform depends on political and social factors, many urban districts seek reform strategies that focus on changes in governance and forget that ultimate real improvement in student learning will depend equally on the development of curricular and instructional changes, changes that require the creation of learning communities through staff development. Thus, many urban districts experiment with privatization, the development of charter schools, and other power-shifting strategies, whereas the creation of a strong system of staff development for current personnel may be a more direct route to school improvement.

Successes in specific schools in several cities have surfaced from time to time and provide hope because those achievements demonstrate that the situation is not hopeless, that inner cities can harbor good schools if people of great energy populate them with ideas and determination. However, systemic reform must take place for districts as units. We cannot tolerate school systems that fail in general while taking comfort in the successes of a few of their units.

Hope comes from several current efforts that demonstrate that systemic school improvement is possible and feasible. Most important, these efforts have radically improved student achievement.

SUCCESS FOR ALL

One such systemic reform effort is the program called "Success for All," directed at the initial years of schooling. Success for All can be compared to an intensive-care medical clinic whose personnel simply refuse to let anybody brought to them give up the ghost without maximum effort. In the case of Success for All, the goal is to be certain that all students receive maximum instructional efforts. "Wellness" is defined as reading adequately by the end of the third grade, so that the students can succeed in the rest of their schooling.

The "vital signs" of student progress, especially in reading, are studied carefully, and tutorial efforts are directed accordingly. The teachers study teaching and learning far more intensively than is typical in most settings. By the end of the third grade, the students' progress in reading approximates the national profile, except that fewer students are significantly below the average than in the average school district.

Success for All made progress from its inception. In its first year, its students did much better than they would have without the program. Progress increased each year, as the intensive diagnostic-prescriptive effort reached larger and larger proportions of its students (Slavin and others 1990). *Any school district that will implement the patterns of Success for All intensively can expect similar progress in as many schools as it chooses to reach.* Intensive leadership, public support—morally and fiscally—and optimism rather than pessimism will be the keys.

Leadership—and moral support by the public—are themes in other systemic initiatives.

THE PITTSBURGH PROGRAM

In Pittsburgh, a very different type of effort generated equally powerful effects, but this time at the secondary level. Richard C.

Wallace, Jr., then superintendent, and his staff designed an extensive districtwide staff development program that tested what can happen when some of the most highly regarded teachers in a large district are concentrated in a high school whose lower SES population has been far below the national average (Wallace, Lemahieu, and Bickel 1990). The Schenley High School became a staff development center where outstanding teachers were brought together. Other district teachers rotated into the school, spending several weeks observing those teachers and studying instruction (Wallace, Lemahieu, and Bickel).

There was a large rise in standardized test scores in eight of nine curriculum areas. In terms of the percentage of students scoring at or above the national average, the rise in total language results was from 27 percent to 61 percent, in reading from 28 percent to 45 percent, in physical science from 21 percent to 63 percent, in biology from 13 percent to 41 percent, and in algebra from 29 percent to 73 percent. The gains were maintained or increased during the second year. As interesting as are the sizes of those improvements, it is equally interesting that they were so immediate. *High schools, and districts, need not feel hopeless about students with poor learning histories.*

Although making large differences in student achievement through school-improvement programs is hardly routine, the number of reports and variety of programs having considerable success suggest that the technology for making rapid and significant change exists. The ones mentioned above are not the only ones. The River City program, described in chapter 2, had substantial and immediate effects. The more effective implementation of Mastery Learning programs (Block and Anderson 1975, Bloom 1984) and Distar (Becker 1977) have generated large results in difficult settings.

FOCUSING THE INNER CITY INQUIRY

We focus our inquiry on the creation of the *capacity to change*. We take the position that change in curriculum and instruction is a necessity and that the capacity to change is partly *technical*—a matter of building good curriculums and the staff development system that will sustain them—and partly *social*—a matter of building an integrated and optimistic organization of teachers and administrators, closely aligned with the energy of the community.

In this segment of our school-renewal journey, we share the specifics of the Inner City Program between 1991 and 1993. We seek to assess what magnitude of change our inner-city schools can absorb, how fast strong initiatives can be implemented, what the effects on students were, and how the social organization responded, changed, and remained the same.

During the first 12 months of implementation, two consultants spent more than 250 days in these schools or in training settings, visited teachers in their classrooms nearly 1,000 times, held countless conferences with teachers and administrators, provided training to over 300 persons, and held seminars on school improvement with about 200 more persons. The level of support during the second year was comparable.

The implementation of the program's seven components was studied in both formal and informal ways. Very specific quantitative data were collected weekly on a sample of the teachers as they tried to implement the components. In addition, observations of their discussions and struggles provided a qualitative picture of responses to the initiatives.

Space does not permit a full ethnographic description of what happened. Following a description of the components of the program, we will present the major findings in terms of lessons learned from each of them. As a way of foreshadowing those findings and giving some perspective on the program as a whole, we offer several unambiguous conclusions from our analysis of the data.

1. Judging from the efforts of Inner City, urban schools can sustain a magnitude of curricular and instructional change far larger than most people suspect. The five inner-city schools changed greatly in ways that affected student learning. The changes were not of the same magnitude in all areas, but each school made great changes.

2. The changes would not have occurred without massive technical support and staff development.

3. The successes did not positively affect the social and organizational climate of the district. Although some people changed greatly—even in the texture of their professional lives—systematic change and ongoing collaborative decision-making did not become major themes in the lives of most of the teachers and administrators. *Concrete evidence that students were learning more and that parents and other community members had become very active helpers did not change the beliefs of most people: they continued to believe that those things could* not *happen!*

4. By the end of the second year, several thousand children were learning more, despite an organizational climate that is a very unlikely setting for positive change. Many students are still learning

more as this paper is written. Gradually, however, things will return to the normalcy of desperate failure.

Nonetheless, we have learned a bit more that can be used in the future as we try to build self-renewing learning communities. Before turning to those lessons, let us tell the story as we see it.

GENERATING INITIATIVES: INCREASING THE CAPACITY OF INNER CITY TO IMPROVE

Essential to school improvement at a systemic level is the optimistic stance that urban schools can develop or absorb substantial innovations—that their existence is not so precarious that the level of reform necessary for perceptible school improvement cannot be generated.

The superintendent of Inner City began with the assumption that systemic reform can be initiated by the district and can interact productively with the energy of school faculties. The superintendent's office then generated a substantial series of initiatives that required strong collaboration between the district's central office and the schools. Whereas many theories of school improvement have emphasized initiatives from one or the other of these two sources—the district or the school—Inner City attempted to develop an approach to school reform that combined the two in appropriate proportions, while avoiding the tension that so often pits the district office against its schools.

The Inner City Initiative for School Improvement was designed directly under the leadership of the superintendent, with planning by teachers and administrators, community members, and members of the board of education. The program of initiatives ran directly in the face of inner-city school problems and their attendant discouragement and skepticism. The initiatives represented a multidimensional attempt to capitalize on what is known from the achievements and failures of the past and were designed to radically change the circumstances in which the children of Inner City schools receive education.

Their designers recognized that unidimensional approaches, however well founded, would not do the job. Many changes needed to occur simultaneously. These changes needed to be valid in their own right, but also needed to transform the district into a moving, self-renewing organization that continuously seeks better ways of educating its children. The community of professional educators needed to be revitalized as part of the effort, so that the urban workplace becomes a desirable place to work and to live. And the educational environment created must propel the children into states of growth far beyond their imagination or that of their observers.

Inner City planners recognized the difficulties they were facing and the problems that have plagued attempts to improve urban schools across the nation. Despite the presence of federal, state, and local initiatives over the last several decades, tests of student achievement confirmed a grim picture in many Inner City schools. Average scores in some classes were as low as the eighth percentile on state norms. In some schools, averages were below the 20th percentile. In most schools, only a handful of students were above the 50th percentile. For nearly all students, the academic picture was dismal.

From the upper-elementary grades through the high schools, much energy was consumed in the management of discipline. As pointed out in a report by the Inner City Commission for Positive Change, a very active coalition of business leaders, a great deal of energy was expended in the enforcement of disciplinary rules. It was not uncommon for the number of suspensions reported by a school during a year to exceed the number of students enrolled.

Awareness of the problems provided a common ground on which the superintendent could generate initiatives to improve the situation. However, there was a "let George do it" attitude on the part of many of the educators, the overcoming of which required great energy.

'DEMONSTRATION' SCHOOLS

The complex of initiatives that formed the Inner City Initiative for School Improvement asked that teachers and administrators learn how to make change happen in many areas. The purpose of the first set of "demonstration" schools was to provide a laboratory within which to figure out how to make the whole set of strategies work and to learn what it would take to support other faculties in the future.

Opportunities to become demonstration schools were offered to the most troubled schools in the district, dependent on a 75 percent approval vote by the faculties. Most of those faculties voted to take on the task of whole school improvement, and five were selected for the program we describe here: four elementary schools and one middle school. The remainder engaged in different programs directed toward the same end. Priority transfers were offered to teachers who dissented strongly, but only two or three teachers took advantage of the offer, and the staffs were stable even through the fourth year.

The initial stages of the program emphasized seven interrelated components: the social organization of the school; the study of teaching and curriculum; the use of technology; the use of tutors; an extended-year schedule; parent involvement; and a cadre of disseminators to support implementation.

Social Organization. Whatever energy is provided by the administration of any district, the schools are the units where actual educational change takes place. Creating faculty synergy is the key. Thus, a major component was the development of a collegial decision-making organization in each school, including leadership teams, study teams, and mechanisms for democratic decision-making on major issues. The faculties were asked to learn how to make the components of the plan work and to generate initiatives that fit the needs of their sites.

The Study of Teaching and Curriculum. All personnel were employed during the first year on extended contracts that provide more than 15 days of training on teaching strategies and curriculum. Models of Teaching that emphasize higher order thinking were the core of the training (Joyce, Weil, and Showers 1992; Joyce and Weil 01996).

Technology. Technology, and especially computer technology, relates to equity in educational opportunity in two ways. First, the computer is beautifully designed for increasing self-teaching capability, especially with respect to access to information and the ability to manage information and with respect to reading and writing and becoming skilled communicators. Second, the computer is an essential tool in today's society. A student who does not possess the technology is disadvantaged in myriad ways, while a student who is computer literate has advantages both in and out of school.

During the first two years, each school received additional computers beyond those stationed in the computer laboratories until all classrooms had computers available to them. Only 20 percent of the faculties of those schools had had *any* experience with computers prior to the inception of the project. Many literally did not know how to turn them on. As part of the technology component and the staff development component, faculties in each school worked to learn how to use their computers in ways that integrate technology with curriculum and teaching strategies.

Tutors. Parents, college students, and military personnel were trained to offer specific services in reading and writing and to give diagnostic reading tests to the students.

Extended Year. During the second year of the initiative, many students received about 20 more days of service than normal.

Parent Involvement. Efforts to enlist the help of parents were extensive. An example is the Just Read and Write program (see chapter 5 for a complete description) that includes communitywide efforts with the goal that each student will read, or be read to, for about an hour each day in addition to his or her school assignments. A "take-home" computer program was also instituted. Families received instruction on the uses of the computer and were given computers to keep in their homes for extended periods. The tutorial program directly involved parents in within-school activities and in the establishment of learning centers in the community.

A Cadre of Disseminators. A cadre of Inner City teachers was recruited and received training on the dissemination of all components of the initiative. This cadre was formed for four primary purposes: (1) to ensure the continuance of the program and to deepen its implementation; (2) to serve as a mechanism for dissemination to other schools; (3) to support implementation of other district efforts, such as the new "core curriculum"; and (4) to increase the internal capability of the district to generate, study, implement, and adapt initiatives, freeing the district from dependence on outside consultants and initiatives.

Any of the seven components listed above would constitute a major school-improvement program. The size of the effort, and its combination of provision of resources and increases in faculty decision-making, made the Inner City Program one of the most thoroughgoing efforts undertaken by any school system. It was not a narrow-gauge strategy, depending on one "quick-fix" scheme for school renewal, but a broad, evolving effort designed to institutionalize better conditions for students and staff alike and to make the system amenable to further efforts generated both by faculties and by system planners.

From a national perspective, the most important issue is that the Inner City Initiative represents a test of the resiliency of inner-city schools: Can these inner-city schools absorb the components described above and integrate and adapt them to their particular circumstances? Thus, the examination of what these schools did and did not do provides some important lessons on school change.

ASSESSING IMPLEMENTATION: LESSONS LEARNED FROM THE EXPERIENCE

A number of lessons were learned during the two years—lessons derived from both successes attained and problems encountered. The first four lessons are general and apply to the entire effort. The remaining lessons relate to specific components. All are derived from a combination of clinical experience with the schools and from data collected on the state of the implementation of the initiatives, combined with information culled from district records.

GENERAL LESSONS

Lesson One: The schools have been able to deal with the complex of initiatives—not perfectly, but in such a way that each of them has made substantial progress in several areas.

Lesson Two: For each initiative, there are some outstanding implementations, ones that have greatly improved the learning environment of the students at school, at home, or both. All schools made progress in the initiative, but the variance was considerable.

Lesson Three: All the initiatives required substantial amounts of technical assistance and facilitation for every school. Faculties were asked to do many things that were new to them. The successes occurred when teachers and administrators set out to learn how to do new things. The lowest levels of implementation occurred where personnel thought they could innovate without having to learn or where insufficient technical assistance was available.

Lesson Four: In the long run, both technical support and facilitation must come from within the district. The emerging cadre of teachers is one possible mechanism, but substantial changes in central-office behavior are needed to utilize such a cadre. Probably a substantial reorganization of central-office personnel is needed. In a large school district, there is a tendency for personnel assigned to the central office to be overwhelmed by the bureaucratic tasks of keeping the system running, and they can quickly lose touch with the schools. Also, they have a tendency to believe that they "know" how to manage change, when in fact very few people have been associated with successful school-improvement efforts.

We believe that all central-office personnel need to be assigned to schools and work part-time in them, probably as teammates with the principals. The central office needs to be a community that studies change and school improvement. This did not happen in Inner City, despite the fact the leadership of the project was centered in the office of the superintendent. The project almost certainly will not last for more than a few years, and the cadre will be used only sporadically and will disband before long.

LESSONS FROM SPECIFIC COMPONENTS

Lesson Five: Just Read and Write. Two of the schools implemented schoolwide efforts; one school developed a program that varies by grade and teacher; and two schools were still learning how to implement Just Read at the end of the third year. *The most successful faculties came to believe that any school can implement Just Read.* The faculties of the other schools believe it just can't be done in their schools. They assign the reason to the character of the community and the children. We believe the reason is that those faculties could not develop the degree of social organization necessary to mount a coordinated effort.

Central-office personnel learned nothing about how to help the schools implement Just Read. They were generally unavailable to participate in the training and support tasks with the consultants. The central-office folks tended to accept the differences in implementation among the schools as effects of differences in the neighborhoods. If a faculty said they could or couldn't do Just Read, the central-office personnel assigned the capability to a predisposition for parents to cooperate or not cooperate. In fact, the demographic differences among schools were small. All the neighborhoods are desperately poor, dangerous places to live, riven by ethnic and racial discord.

Because Just Read emphasizes reading at home, there has probably been a substantial change in the home life of the children where it was well implemented. According to baseline data, nearly all the children did not read at home *at all* before the program was established. Students at one of the successful schools celebrated the reading of 30,000 books during the last 6 months of its first-year implementation (an average of 40 per child). In addition, kindergarten children took home a book each night for their parents to read to them, which made radical changes in the adult-child relationships in the beginning school year. Based on earlier studies of Just Read, each child in this school read several times more books each year, on average, than did the average child from school districts serving the children from much higher SES homes.

In a second school's successful implementation, 20,000 books were read, more than 20 per child, during a 6-month period.

In the school with uneven implementation, reading at home ranged from an average of more than 10 books per month for each student in one class (the *average* child in that class was reading nearly 100 books per year, nearly all of them at home) to virtually no books in several classes. The uneven implementation was instructive: the low-implementing teachers believed that the parents would not cooperate, despite the fact that those same parents or their neighbors were cooperating with the teacher across the hall. In fact, if the low-implementing teachers simply tried the process, the amounts of at-home reading by their students would rise quickly.

Lesson Six: Tutoring. This is another component where implementation varied widely. The most important lesson here is from one school that demonstrated that neighborhood parents and others can be recruited, trained, and organized to the point where about 500 of its 950 students experienced daily tutoring for at least one six-week period.

Some of the other schools made substantial progress with tutoring, but did not achieve the same level of implementation as did the school referred to above *despite the fact that the tutoring was regarded as a success by the faculties.* In the low-implementing schools, an effort to recruit and train tutors would be made, appear to be making headway, and then be allowed to languish until the consultants persuaded the principals and faculties to revive the initiative again. Looking back, we believe that successful implementation of the tutoring component requires direct leadership by the principal, assisted by other personnel who are willing to make aggressive contact with the parents and community. Their efforts must be accompanied by an extensive orientation of all faculty members about the purposes of the program and the most effective techniques for using the tutors.

The central-office personnel stood aloof from the tutoring program. Most of them did not believe that parents in these neighborhoods could be recruited as tutors, partly because they believe there are too few parents who are both interested and literate. The fact that some schools did so well with the tutoring component did not change these beliefs.

Lesson Seven: Take-Home Computers. Two school faculties implemented exceptional "take-home" programs and demonstrated what can be done with two very different approaches. One school purchased a number of portable Macintoshes and worked out a system to recruit and train parents, who then received computers for several weeks, after which another group of parents were cycled into the process. Eight training cycles were completed. Altogether, about a quarter of the student body of nearly 1,200 had a computer in the home for six to eight weeks during the school year.

Parents and children were enthusiastic. The program made contact with a large number of parents who previously were isolated from the school. Importantly, all the computers are still intact and operating, despite the fears of many persons who felt that they would be damaged, lost, or stolen.

The second take-home approach employed the "Josten" program, which was modified to be similar to the program described above, except that the Josten organization conducted the training and maintained the computers. Six- to eight-week cycles were maintained for about 20 computers. Parents literally stood in line for the opportunity to participate. Altogether, about 180 of the 1,000 students in this school, plus their siblings and parents, had a computer at home for one of the cycles.

The take-home component appears to be viable. *The successes indicate that it can be implemented, will increase parent involvement, and is popular with all concerned.* Both of the success stories were in schools with populations generally thought to be very difficult to reach. The knowledge exists to implement it in any school.

Unfortunately, central-office staff who could work with other school faculties to implement a similar program did not study what was happening. From its initiation, they dismissed the take-home program as a viable component of the school-renewal initiative because they believed the computers would be stolen. Evidence to the contrary had no effect on their beliefs. After two years of success, without loss of a single computer, central-office personnel expressed the same opinions they held at the beginning.

Lesson Eight: Computers for In-School Use. The technology initiative refurbished the schools' computer laboratories and provided computers and "teacher work stations" in the classrooms. This initiative significantly upgraded the use of technology by Inner City students.

To appreciate the initiative fully, one needs to assess the state of computer use in the schools before it was made. One school had *no* computer use at all when the initiative began. For technical reasons, its computer lab was out of service, and only two or three of its teachers knew *anything* about the computer as a device, let alone how to use it instructionally. One school had a lab, with a well-qualified director, that served the students once each week, but only two or three of the other teachers were acquainted with the instructional uses of computers. Two other schools were in about the same shape as that one, but their labs did not function as well. There was only one school, which had several ongoing computer projects, where a majority of the faculty were computer users and where half of the classrooms had computers for use during the regular instructional day.

Now, all the computer laboratories have been upgraded, and most of the students in all five schools have competence in word-processing and some other basic computer functions. Nearly all the teachers have knowledge of the computer and basic instructional functions related to it. About one-fifth of the teachers make some use of workstations and panels that permit large-group instruction, and databases on CD ROM disks are coming into use.

Much remains to be done. Many problems have to be solved before it can be said that every child will be computer literate and that all teachers will be using the available technology effectively for instruction. However, these five schools went from far below the national average in computer technology to average, or above the nation's average, in one short year. In passing, we note that the accomplishment in this area is a real student-achievement gain, albeit one not currently measured by state or national testing programs. Computer literacy is a legitimate student-achievement goal, whether or not it increases achievement in the traditional core areas of the curriculum.

Lesson Nine: The Extended Year. All five schools implemented this component. Perhaps the most interesting information comes from the effort of the middle school. Its teachers, led by two or three who have become outstanding instructional leaders, created a curriculum that includes cross-disciplinary instruction, team teaching, lengthened instructional periods, and active models of teaching. At the end of the second year, nearly one-third (160) of the students were participating. Parent and student demand for the program has been excellent, and parent involvement in enrolling students has been far above expectations—another plus for the overall program, bringing parents closer to the school and involving them more actively in promoting the education of their children.

Lesson Ten: The Study of Instruction. Not without difficulty, the faculties of each of the five schools were assembled and received instruction on several models of teaching designed to generate cooperative classrooms, involve students actively in productive and creative thinking, and increase student achievement in general.

Following the general training, faculties were organized into study groups to implement these instructional methods and study their effects on student learning.

Faculties differed widely in their patterns of implementation, and use of the teaching strategies varied considerably within each school. One school developed its own cadre of teachers who studied the teaching models and then offered training to their colleagues. From a socioprofessional point of view, this school's method has many advantages. Nevertheless, implementation is a slow process, even in this school, though it may be that the institutionalization of the study of teaching may endure in such a collaborative setting.

The middle school reached the point where about 15 percent of its instructional time was generated through the study of new teaching strategies, but individual faculty use varied from regular and consistent use to almost no use. Student achievement, indicated by grades, varied according to the level of teacher implementation. The students of the high- and middle-implementation teachers received grades at the end of the second year 0.3 higher than the students of the lowest implementing teachers. The students of the high-implementation teachers received an average grade of 2.02 compared to an average grade of 1.72 for students in the classes of the low-using teachers. Using grades as a criterion, achievement rose in the classrooms of the low-using teachers. Before the initiatives, the "average grade" for the whole school was below 1.50.

In one elementary school, the kindergarten through grade 2 teachers were the highest users, the grade 3 to 5 teachers were uneven (some high and some low users), and the grade 6 teachers rarely used the new teaching strategies. In this school, CTBS scores were available for the spring 1992 and spring 1993 testing periods, and the patterns of student scores directly reflect the patterns of teacher implementation of the teaching strategies.

The grade 1 and 2 scores indicate a dramatic upward trend. In terms of median scores, they are as follows:

FOR GRADE 1:

- In reading, the 1993 first-grade median score was at the 41st percentile of the state, compared to the 20th percentile in 1992.
- In "total language," the 1993 median was at the 48th percentile, compared to the 27th in 1992.
- In mathematics, the 1993 median was at the 44th percentile, compared with the 29th in 1992.

FOR GRADE 2:

- In reading, the 1993 median was at the 23rd percentile, compared with the 9th percentile in 1992.
- In "total language," the 1993 median was at the 19th percentile, compared with the 5th in 1992.
- In mathematics, the 1993 median was at the 42nd percentile, compared with the 8th in 1992.

FOR GRADES 3 TO 5:

- The overall results were not significantly different between 1992 and 1993, though some classes showed an upward trend and others showed a downward trend.

FOR GRADE 6:

- The results revealed a decline of about 20 percentile points in each of the three areas (reading, total language, and mathematics).

Implementation is the key. Powerful instructional strategies, *when implemented*, produce student achievement. The high-implementation classrooms made progress in student achievement in the first year of the initiatives. The grade 1 students in the school whose data are referred to above were approximately average for the state in 1993 and thus began their school life with an even break. The second-graders were on the move also. Whether this trend continues will depend on strong efforts to achieve implementation across the grades and classes.

LESSONS FOR THE NEXT TIME AROUND

Substantial changes have been brought about. The example of Inner City demonstrates that curricular initiatives can be made rapidly when a district breaks away from the usual set of school-improvement strategies and generates initiatives that school faculties can pick up and implement with respect to their situations. Inner-city schools, despite their problems, are not fragile. They can make many changes rapidly.

School faculties will implement initiatives variably, but as the spectrum in Inner City reveals, they can do outstanding work, and, when properly nurtured, they can rapidly change dismal records of student learning in some of our toughest educational settings. "Success for All," the Schenley initiative, the River City program, and now the Inner City program are all demonstrating what can be done and be done quickly.

However, such changes do not create a self-renewing organization. The development of a coherent plan and evidence of successes had a negligible effect on the attitudes of many teachers and administrators and the way they conduct business. Successes in implementing components such as Just Read, tutoring, or the take-home computer program did not alter the beliefs or behaviors of central-office personnel, and student-achievement gains did not affect them either.

Information indicating lack of success of a program or practice did not affect behavior either. Instead of saying, "This area needs more attention," the tendency was to give up on the area. For example, the attitude "Can't do anything with sixth graders. It's just too late to help them" had become culturally acceptable both to express and to practice. Essentially, we believe that there is a culture of failure, of hopelessness, in which some school faculties as organizations operate much like individuals with poor self-concepts.

Many school-improvement strategies have tried to affect the organization by concentrating on changing governance structures. We believe that democracy is essential, as are the creation of clear initiatives accompanied by strong technical assistance and staff development. However, the kind of democracy created in a culture of failure is likely to be a perverse and negative one.

We believe the school-improvement process needs to concentrate on the study of the social dynamic of the organization and on the attitudes generated by it, so that people can take hold of the negativism that presently dominates some settings and build the kind of climate that engenders self-actualization. As most schools-as-organizations are structured and most programs of staff development conducted, high achievements and successes fade away as the adults strive to survive psychologically in an environment that is very hard for them to live in. It may be that we will have to create a corps of social therapists to continue the inquiry into school renewal, but if we have to do so, let's get on with it.

SUMMARY AND COMMENTARY

The history of inner-city schools in the United States has been a tragedy for several decades. Administrative initiatives, such as the categorical programs, have not ameliorated the situation very much. Yet we have ample evidence that intensive school-improvement programs can make a big difference in the lives of students. The tragedy now would be to deny the successes that have been achieved or to believe that their lessons are not pertinent because they were not "perfect" programs.

And, let's remember, our kids need to be placed first. Currently, adult concerns and negative attitudes about what is possible for our children overwhelm the successes, so that successes with children in classrooms, schools, and districts across this country do not stand out as beacons to guide further efforts.

So, what's our final lesson from Inner City at this point in our school-renewal journey? The urban schools can do it! Reform, that is. Ron Edmonds' ringing question "How many do you have to see?" and his assertion that real change will be more a matter of political and social will are clearer and clearer as truths.

Now, let's move into our last story, of a school/university collaborative where shared decision-making, student learning, and action research were the unifying actions for participation.

ACTION NETWORK

In a Southeastern state, the faculties of 60 schools worked to build shared governance and generate schoolwide action research. Technical assistance was provided to leadership teams through workshops, an information-retrieval system, and a yearly onsite visit. For six years, the progress of schools in Action Network has been studied.

The successful schools made schoolwide initiatives during their first year of participation and learned to study the effects on student learning early in the process. Schools that did not cohere early tended to become "stuck." Not surprisingly, principal leadership was critical in changing governance and establishing the action-research process. Changes in leadership could adversely affect the process very quickly even after schools had been doing well for several years.

Nearly all the most successful schools drew on external technical assistance in governance and action research. The importance of technical assistance is so great that fairly accurate predictions of success can be made by knowing whether schools do or do not reach out for and find experienced consultants and form an extensive and intensive relationship with them.

CHAPTER 6

THE ACTION NETWORK: ACTION RESEARCH ON ACTION RESEARCH

EMILY CALHOUN AND LEW ALLEN

Some of us believe that schoolwide action research is a full-service model for school renewal. To test this belief, we look at what happens in schools that are seriously engaged in conducting action research. What areas are selected for exploration by the faculty as a unit? What do faculties do with the schoolwide action-research process? Does collective inquiry by teachers and administrators develop in a deep, meaningful way? Does collective inquiry foster increases in individual inquiry? Do changes occur in the educational environment, and, if so, do those changes affect student learning, and in what manner? These are a few of the questions we investigate as we conduct action research within the Georgia League of Professional Schools.

In this chapter we report the findings from several years of study of the approximately 60 member schools of the League. We reflect on the interaction between action research and the culture of schooling, report the results of our attempts to improve technical assistance to schools adopting action research as their route to school renewal, and make recommendations for future study and practice.

As you follow our inquiry, you will find many instances of success, both in making changes in the workplace and in making initiatives that have positive effects on students. What we most hope to share, however, are the increments of insight we have had into the nature of the cultural change necessary if schools are to become learning communities for educators as well as for students. Our understanding is limited, but our five-year inquiry has given us a clearer focus on the cultural frameworks—the perceptual lenses—that teachers and administrators use as they approach school improvement. We also see more clearly the ways those lenses change as inquiry-based school renewal is achieved.

THE NATURE OF SCHOOLWIDE ACTION RESEARCH

Schoolwide action research is, at the core, simply cooperative, disciplined inquiry by school faculties acting as a collective. A group of people, in this case the staff of an educational institution, try to improve practice in a fashion that borrows some of the tools of the behavioral sciences and puts them to work in the service of the school. The group studies the environment, focusing particularly on student learning as a product of curriculum and instruction. Hypotheses are developed in the form of theses about how particular changes in the learning environment will help the students learn better. The changes are made and the effects studied. Then, the process is repeated.

When the process is well established, faculties have created a self-renewing organization that supports their future work and their study of its effects on the lives of students. And the educational environment has changed not only for the students but for the faculty as well. The Georgia League and its school faculties strive to work in this manner to change their workplace and generate informed democratic action for school renewal.

HISTORICAL PERSPECTIVE ON ACTION RESEARCH FOR ORGANIZATIONAL CHANGE

Fifty years ago Kurt Lewin, who generated the early formulations of action research to improve organizations, and Stephen Corey, who was the chief advocate for the use of action research in education, knew that cultural change would occur from the process and, indeed, had to occur if the process were to succeed (Lewin 1947, 1948; Corey 1953). They knew that most organizations could not conduct good action research (or successfully absorb or adapt to technological changes) unless the culture of the organization was changed by the process, enabling innovation to occur. They believed that persons working in and responsible for organizations were not using data to inform practice or engaging in collective study of the goals of the organization.

Lewin and Corey promoted action research not just to help industry and education become more efficient and effective, but because they wished to change the status quo of behaviors and interactions within the organization and to break the cycles of inertia by creating an entirely different kind of organization. For the benefit of both workers and clients, Lewin and Corey wanted our schools and other institutions to develop a culture of continuous study and self-renewal.

This continuous, collective inquiry is the core of the self-renewing organization; yet creating inquiry-oriented schools has been difficult. There are powerful internal and external forces that lead people to accept schools as they are and to support the status quo, however unsuccessful it may be for many students and staff members. It is easy to see how such attitudes might discourage educators from innovating.

Cultural control operates from within the walls of the school and from without. Many citizens would say schools were invented for the transmission of the primary culture, for control of youth, and for ensuring acquaintance with long-valued content. These beliefs about the purposes of schools and this readiness to accept how they are operated have been amazingly stable across the years among both educators and the general public. We must ask ourselves if this stability has inhibited the development of healthy dissonance necessary for changing behavioral norms. As uncomfortable as it is to say, collective inquiry, including the study of teaching and learning, is an innovation that assaults the norms of most schools.

Past and present action-research scholars provide conceptual structures that the members of an organization can use to work together and carry out inquiry (Lewin; Corey; Glickman 1990; Calhoun 1994; Ainscow, Hopkins, and West 1994). However, *the focus of the inquiry is up to the members of each organization*, making it a self-determining, "inside-out" strategy for school improvement. Nevertheless, phrases like "inside-out," "bottom-up," "teacher empowerment," and "site-based decision-making" do not quite capture the reality of what faculties in League schools experience as schoolwide action research encounters the traditional norms of the culture of schooling.

ACTION RESEARCH AS A WAY OVER OR THROUGH OBSTACLES TO SCHOOL RENEWAL

Schoolwide action research is a strategy for "school-based" or "site-based" school improvement. However, the literature on action research emphasizes processes for making synchronous changes in both the culture of the school and the process of education. Much of the literature on the site-based movement emphasizes the removal of organizational barriers to change, with the thesis that cultural and curricular/instructional quality will improve as a consequence. The implicit argument is that teachers already have the skills and tools to build a better organization and to educate students more effectively and that they will exercise these tools once the offending constraints are removed.

An oft-heard comment related to school-based-improvement strategies such as action research goes something like this: "If school improvement were just turned over to the folks in each school, inhibitions to school improvement would disappear, and schools and the education of students could improve immediately." We have two serious misgivings about the assumptions underpinning such comments.

First, we do not believe that teachers and principals are currently withholding their competence classroom by classroom or school by school. We believe that most teachers and principals are engaging in the best practices in their current repertoire, and we believe that teachers currently have more control over instruction, the major factor schools have control over for improving student learning, than anyone else in the educational system.

Second, the rhetoric surrounding the "turn it all over to the schools" stance generally recommends fewer constraints on practice, changes in the unhealthy work setting, and more power for teachers; relatively little is said about *how* to help faculties transform themselves from "what is" to "what can be." Despite the clamor of numerous reform movements, normative behaviors in classrooms and schools have been very stable for at least the last 30 years. Promising initiatives—whether they originated at the school, the district, the state, or the national level—have often dissolved as they encountered these norms (Goodlad and Klein 1970, Lortie 1975, Little 1982, Goodlad 1984, David and Peterson 1984, Stiegelbauer and Anderson 1992, Muncey and McQuillan 1993).

In the "real world" of school and district implementation, schoolwide action research *collides* with the traditional norms of the culture of schooling: *a faculty that chooses the action-research route will find that the norms that govern professional interaction will change radically and that part of the challenge of school renewal is to use the structure of the action-research process to generate new cultural norms around teaching and learning.*

As faculties agree to engage in action research, they need to understand that they are actually asking themselves to change. Many of us want better schools, but think it will happen if *others* change: students, colleagues, principals, district-office personnel, parents, the community. Or, we look for new structures that will make the difference: new discipline codes, new ways of scheduling, different ways of assessing performance. Essentially, we look *around* ourselves, whereas *we are the ones who have to change if student learning is to be affected.*

If educational history provides any guidance, there are no comprehensive programs, no encompassing innovations, no degree of strategic planning, and no amount of money that will bring about the schools that many of us want. Only changes in *our* behavior will create better learning/living places for our students and for ourselves. Thus, to embrace action research is to embrace growth for ourselves.

Faculties as societies are no different from other social groups in that they have mechanisms, albeit tacit ones, for protecting the normative patterns that regulate interaction and make life predictable for their members. An important normative feature of schools is privatism. Despite the existence of curriculum guides and the contemporary processes in most school districts for involving large numbers of teachers in the writing of those guides, ultimately the curriculum— what is taught and how it is taught—is the province of teachers working alone.

To embrace *schoolwide* action research is to agree that the faculty will create a democratic decision-making organization in which everyone is involved in collecting, analyzing, and sharing information; thinking through directions for actions; acting; and examining the effects. Deciding to embrace democracy is a decision to exchange the individualistic norms within which most schools have operated for the norms of collective decision-making and collective action. Thus, to tell the story of the introduction of action research to a school is to describe an attempt to rebuild the normative structures of the small societies we call school faculties.

THE GEORGIA LEAGUE: PREMISES AND OPERATIONS

The Georgia League of Professional Schools is a school/university collaborative formed to support school renewal. In 1989, the Program for School Improvement at the University of Georgia invited schools throughout the state to join a self-governed affiliation of schools held together by common goals and processes (Glickman, Allen, and Lunsford 1994). Schools volunteer to join. Schools interested in affiliating with the League send a team that includes building administrators, teachers (the majority), and, if the team wishes, representatives from their district office, to a two-day orientation and planning workshop.

The workshop focuses on shared governance, teaching and learning, and action research. The rationale for each operational premise is explained. For example, *shared governance* or democratic decision-making is used to tap the collective wisdom resident onsite in any school and the collective energy needed to bring about major school change. *Student learning and instruction* are emphasized because "teaching" is the major work of the school. And *action research* is the mechanism for making a problem-solving approach to life a normal way of doing business in schools for the benefit of both educators and students. If, after the workshop, team members believe that affiliation with the League can help their school move forward, they take this information back to the staff at their school.

A school is accepted into the League when 80 percent of its faculty have voted (by secret ballot) to join. In their letter of application for membership, representatives of the school sign a commitment letter that specifies activities university staff agree to provide and activities the school agrees to pursue (shared governance, instructional initiatives that promote student learning, and action research). Despite this process, faculties vary greatly in the extent to which they recognize the cultural implications of the journey they are beginning. For many faculty members, the reality of action research doesn't become clear until they have engaged in it.

The university commits to provide five services to League members:

1. Four days of meetings during each membership year, primarily focused on shared decision-making and the conduct of action research, including the sharing of progress by the schools.

2. An Information Retrieval System that provides articles, research information, and resource connections.
3. A "network exchange" newsletter.
4. Telephone consultations with League staff.
5. A one-day, onsite visit by a facilitator. The visit is followed by a report to the school that describes the facilitator's perception of the current status of shared governance in the school, its focus on student learning and instruction, and action research in the school.

In addition, schools have free access to summer institutes on team building and action research and additional onsite consultations, which some schools actively seek. (See Calhoun and Glickman 1993 and Calhoun and Allen 1994 for an overview of the technical support in action research provided to League schools.)

As of January 1995, the League included 60 elementary and secondary schools in Georgia. Eighteen of these 60 schools have been League members for 5 years; 17 for 4 years; 16 for 3 years; and nine for 1 year. Resulting from deliberations by the League Congress about the use of resources and the nature of colleagueship within the League, membership was closed for 1993-94 but opened again in 94-95.

School faculties tend to rejoin the League. Current members include 75 percent of the schools that joined the League in 1990, 81 percent of the schools that joined in 1991, and 80 percent of the schools that joined the League in 1992. (See Appendix, Table A-1, for membership figures for 1990-94.)

Although the Program for School Improvement at the University of Georgia initiated the League, representatives from the schools have been organized to take over its governance. The members of this representative group, called the Congress, now determine the services that are provided, develop policies, and set membership fees (stable at $1,000 per year per school).

ACTION RESEARCH FOR SCHOOL RENEWAL AS SUPPORTED IN THE LEAGUE

The focus is on improvement in three domains. One is the betterment of the organization's problem-solving ability. With repeated cycles of action research, the faculty as a collegial group learns to work together to identify problems and solve them. Second is improvement in curriculum and instruction. Third is equity for students through schoolwide implementation. For example, if the faculty studies the writing process in order to offer better instructional opportunities for students, the intent is that all students benefit, not just those taught by a few faculty members. Thus, in an area of common concern or interest, every classroom and every teacher are involved in collective study and regular assessment of effects on students. As they strive for schoolwide growth, faculty members may involve students and parents, and even the general community, in data collection and interpretation and in the selection of options for action.

The collective inquiry roughly follows this cyclical pattern: *The faculty selects the area of interest or concern; collects, organizes, and interprets onsite and external data related to this area; and takes action based on this information* (Calhoun 1991, Glickman 1990). The phases of the process overlap inherently. Action researchers constantly retrace their steps and revisit earlier phases before (or while) going forward again. This collective inquiry into the work of school professionals (teaching) and its effects on students (learning and development) is a "rolling," cyclical process that serves as formative evaluation of initiatives undertaken by the school community (Calhoun 1994).

The collective decision to select an area of focus and to develop a data-collection process in the chosen area is an essential element of the action-research process and one that involves a considerable change in practice. Collectively exploring a substantive area of the teaching/learning process generates social and technical problems in most schools. To move forward with their exploration and their vision of what is possible, faculties have to solve problems. For example, each faculty must learn how to work together as a collective unit, learn how to select just one or two areas for common study from among the many possible areas of focus, learn how to use the varied perspectives that individuals bring to the exploration, and learn how to select from among the many possible tools available to support disciplined inquiry.

In most American schools, each teacher alone assesses his or her students' progress through the year. Formative evaluation of progress as a collective activity of the faculty is rare. Standardized tests are used by many faculties and leadership teams for summative evaluation, but even the results of those are not analyzed intensively or diagnostically and hence are not used for decision-making by the faculty as a collective body. To conduct action research for school renewal, faculties need to structure routines for continuous data collection and interpretation of those data to analyze progress and make informed decisions.

The introduction of these uses of information involves a continuous confrontation with data in a fashion that changes normative practice. For instance, consider what happens when a faculty concentrates for a while on disciplinary actions. Teachers gather data on referrals, detentions, and suspensions for a live, week-to-week examination. Then they take action to reduce the amount of energy spent on control through punitive actions. The result is that they have structured part of their work time to look at data in an area of common concern. *Traditionally, these regular encounters with the current status of behavior and performance and the regular reports of progress or lack of it have been more common by teachers as individuals; they are uncommon by teachers working as faculties.*

The collective nature of schoolwide action research may require individuals to reconcile previously unexplored differences. One of the silent joys of working alone for many of us is that "we are in charge," and even if we are not in complete control of what happens, we are at least "in charge of what it means." Whether behind the classroom door or office door or as an individual teacher-researcher, when we are working alone or as sole "adult," we have little disagreement about the interpretation of the data, the explanation of the results, or the instructional or curricular actions we decide to take.

In contrast, when working with colleagues, we must deal with other individuals who have their interpretations of data, their own explanations, and their ideas about actions to take. Some of these interpretations, explanations, and actions will be similar to ours; others may be radically different. Part of learning how to conduct action research—and how to live as a community—is how to proceed with collective action when our perceptions and our ideas about promising actions are not congruent with those of our colleagues.

Here is a case in point. Recently, we observed a school where the faculty "discovered" that reports of "tardiness" approached 300 a day in a student population of 800. Those "demerits" accumulated into penalties that included more than 100 suspensions from school each year.

Confronted with those data, the faculty realized the amount of cumulative energy they were expending and the sizable loss of instructional time by so many students. Reaction and concern were inevitable. Members offered proposals ranging from a Draconian increase in penalties to a verbal campaign that confronted the students with the problem. Some faculty members wanted to "do nothing," believing that the situation was just a product of human nature.

When a campaign was mounted and "tardies" dropped almost immediately to about 50 per day, the faculty was "confronted" with success and collective efficacy. Again, there were different interpretations of the success. Some, believing that total success was possible, wanted to redouble the efforts and strive to reduce tardies to zero. Some, believing the problem had been solved, wanted to stop the initiative. Some, angry that they had been proved wrong, wanted to ventilate their frustration.

This "data-confrontation" process, conflicting as it does with the normative ways of doing business, can generate discomfort until faculties become accustomed to using it as part of their "reality check" on what is happening in their school and on the effects of actions they are taking. However, unless the confrontation-with-data routine gets established, problem definition is virtually impossible, making the selection of actions haphazard and the tracking of progress a matter of impressions rather than a healthy examination of what is, or is not, being accomplished.

As we study action research in League schools, the task of selecting an area for collective exploration; the processes of data collection, interpretation, and use; and the actions and innovations selected for collective pursuit have important places in our inquiry.

The remainder of this chapter is a brief overview of the study of action research in League schools, summaries of findings in response to the three guiding questions listed below, shared thoughts about the magnitude of the tasks action-research schools face culturally, results of action-research studies that sought to apply the findings of the earlier League studies, and suggestions for facilitating schoolwide action research.

THE STUDY OF ACTION RESEARCH IN LEAGUE SCHOOLS

For five years, beginning with the inception of the League in 1990, the staff at the University of Georgia has conducted a formative study of the development of the action-research process in its member schools and shared the results with university and school personnel and the larger professional community.

GUIDING QUESTIONS

The "big" question we study is "How are schools using action research?" This question, in turn, encompasses many "smaller" questions: Does it get implemented? Do parts of it get implemented? What causes problems? Do schools that are more successful with it share common characteristics? Are faculties implementing the technical and social innovations that are blended into the action-research process? Does action research become a series of collective activities to be checked off a list or does it become part of routine collective inquiry around common goals and concerns?

Because data collection and analysis are essential parts of action-research, our first League study on action research (Calhoun 1991) focused on the types of data collected by schools and how they used this information. In the second study (Calhoun 1992), we continued to examine data collection but expanded the scope to include the behaviors of faculties. The third study (Calhoun and Glickman 1993) focused on successes, difficulties, and concerns that arise as school staff learn to use onsite data and information from the literature to select collective actions and assess effects. The fourth study (Calhoun and Allen 1994) focused on the effects of action research on students and on the cultural environment of the school.

In the next few pages, findings from these four studies are gathered around three questions. Responses to Questions 1 and 2 relate primarily to what happened during the action-research process; responses to Question 3 relate primarily to the effects of action research on students.

1. What do faculties select as an area for collective exploration or improvement?
2. What has been the nature of data collection and utilization?
3. What are the effects on students?

SOURCES OF DATA

Three primary data sources were used in each of the four studies. The action plans generated by the schools constituted one source. The second consisted of reports by university-based and school-based facilitators, especially the reports developed from interviews conducted during visits to the sites and observations of meetings held during those visits. The third was made up of documents provided by the schools, such as examples of data they collected and shared. Secondary sources included records from League files on the use of the information-retrieval system; records of attendance at meetings and workshops; files of queries for information; and proceedings from meetings.

For each year's study cited above, all three types of primary data relevant to the major foci of the investigation have been available for about 80 percent of the schools. However, the amount and quality of data are somewhat uneven. The amount and depth of information provided by the schools vary considerably. Also, even though facilitators use standardized protocols, interview questions, and outlines for the onsite visits and reports, the facilitators are not "standard issue" and the opportunity to collect data varies from place to place and visit to visit.

Over the years, the technical, analytical work of the League research team has been largely a matter of a series of content analyses of the three primary data sources and of archival data and protocols from interviews and observations beyond those collected during the onsite visits.

We discuss what we are finding and ask clarifying questions of one another and of our colleagues in the schools. Then we do more counting and reflection. *We are engaged in action research;* therefore, we are especially interested in information indicating changes needed in immediate practice and in forming hypotheses to test through future League actions. At regular intervals, we try to stand back from it all—from the daily activities of keeping everything going and from the specifics of our data—and figure out where we are in this inquiry and what we are learning about school renewal and about ourselves as facilitators.

CHARACTERISTICS OF THE SCHOOLS

Tables A-2, A-3, and A-4 in the Appendix provide basic demographic data. With respect to each characteristic—location, size, percentage of students receiving wholly or partly subsidized lunches, and percentage of "minority" students—there is a considerable range. League schools are urban, rural, and suburban; are large and small; contain various proportions of minorities; and serve many combinations of economic strata.

Moreover, one characteristic does not predict another. The economically poor and minorities are distributed among the urban, rural, and suburban areas. There are large elementary schools and small high schools. Within the League, one cannot predict the characteristics of the next member by examining these data, but one can predict that the next 10 members will represent many demographic patterns.

The schools whose experiences are shared in the following findings joined the League as cohort groups in 1990, 1991, and 1992.

SUMMARY OF FINDINGS ON THE ACTION-RESEARCH PROCESS

These findings are organized around three topics: (1) selecting a common goal or priority area for study, (2) the nature of data collection and use, and (3) the effects on students.

SELECTING AREAS FOR COMMON STUDY

The focus on student learning through the study of curriculum and instruction was stressed during the initial orientation provided to help League schools decide whether to join, was reiterated in the letter of commitment signed by a representative of the school, and has been emphasized throughout the technical-assistance process.

League staff encourage faculties to select an area or concern that relates directly to student learning and that has strong face validity—one behind which almost every faculty member would affirm, "Yes, this is critically important for us to study." In this section we discuss the selection of areas of focus during the first four years of membership.

This information on Phase 1 of the action-research process was gleaned largely from the action plans developed by 52 of the 54 member schools during the 1993-94 school year. The analysis of the action plans was confirmed in general by the analysis of the reports developed by the facilitators. The 52 schools had been members from two to four years. Insufficient information was available from the other two schools.

For 1993-94, 24 of the 52 schools were focusing directly on student learning or on changes in curriculum/instruction. They were emphasizing one of three areas of emphasis: student learning goals, such as "improving the quality of student writing" (composition), changes in instruction, such as "implementing whole language"; and changes in curriculum, such as "designing new units in mathematics." Here is the distribution of schools across these three focus areas:

- Student learning goals—11 school faculties expressed the focus of their collective work in terms of investigating/changing some aspect of *student learning or performance.*
- Changes in instruction—10 school faculties expressed the focus of their collective work in terms of changing some aspect of *instruction.*
- Changes in curriculum—three school faculties expressed the focus of their collective work in terms of developing or refining some aspect of *curriculum.*

The stated foci for the other 28 schools varied considerably. Many had to do (1) with aspects of the climate of the school—such as communication within the school, student motivation, developing statements of core values, or creating a positive environment; (2) with administrative matters such as scheduling; and (3) with developing provisions for inclusion of special-education students.

Some of the schools that emphasized student-learning goals also selected a common initiative to try to achieve gains, but more frequently individuals and small groups selected their own initiatives, so that a diverse, rather than unified, approach resulted.

Changes in curriculum and instruction were related to student learning in about half the schools where the focus was on curriculum and instruction. In the other half of the schools where faculties were studying curriculum and instruction, the initiative itself was stated as the goal (for example, "to implement cooperative learning"), but there were no plans to collect data about the implementation of the initiative or student responses to it.

Summary—Selection of Foci. Across four years, about one-fourth of the League schools were able to establish a common student-learning goal during their first year; about one-fourth more during their second year; and a few more during the third year. The remainder set goals and initiatives in areas peripheral to student learning. Some of those eventually would leave the League.

The schools that made the most progress in using action research to study student learning or curriculum and instruction focused their goal(s) and/or initiative(s) around these areas early on—in their first year of membership in the League. School faculties who set their priorities in the general areas of climate, communication, or scheduling in their first year were slow in moving toward curriculum and instruction or student-learning goals in their second, third, or fourth year.

COLLECTING, ORGANIZING, AND USING ONSITE DATA AND EXTERNAL INFORMATION

Each League faculty determines the questions it wishes to explore. The methodology used may be simple quantitative methods such as counting instances of referrals and grades, more complex quantitative methods including the disaggregation of data on achievement by gender and race/ethnicity, short-term qualitative studies of student behavior, multiyear case studies, and combinations of short- and long-term quantitative and qualitative methods.

When orienting the schools about data collection, the university staff presented a variety of data sources and ways of handling information. Without deprecating the use of standardized tests, the staff pointed out that tracking student learning in a formative manner required the use of information that could be collected regularly during the school year, rather than once a year as a summation. The staff suggested that regularly collected "existing" data—such as grades, the results of curriculum-relevant tests, information about disciplinary action, samples of writing, and other information that is available in most schools—be mined and used to identify needs and track progress. In addition, the staff recommended exploring "creative" means of studying the students, such as through student-generated products, problem-solving activities, and cooperative endeavors.

The first question explored here is whether the faculties studied student achievement and, if so, by what means. The presentation of these data begins with schools who became members the first year of the League and then proceeds to those who joined later, while continuing to follow the "charter" group. Table 6.1 presents data for 24 schools that joined the League in 1990. These data were taken from a content analysis of their action-research plans and facilitator reports. (In 1991, two of these schools—one elementary and one high school—decided not to renew their membership.)

In January/February of their first year of membership, eight, or one-third, of the schools specified the collection of student-achievement data as part of their action plans. By the end of the first year, 12 schools, or about half, specified the use of student-achievement data, and that number remained essentially unchanged during the second year. Data sources cited included standardized test data, letter grades in courses, failure rates, overage/eligibility rosters, and standardized assessments of reading and writing (for example, using basal tests or state criterion-referenced test results). Schools entering the League later behaved similarly: about one-half came to study student achieve-

T A B L E   6.1

CITATIONS IN ACTION PLANS OF USE OF STUDENT-
ACHIEVEMENT DATA OF THE 24 ORIGINAL LEAGUE
MEMBERS DURING THEIR FIRST TWO YEARS

Dates of Action Plans

	Jan/Feb 1990	May 1990	Feb 1991	May 1991
	*N=24	N=24	N=21	N=22
Schools	8	13	12	13

* N indicates the number of school action plans available for analysis.

ment by some means during the year, and the number did not rise much during the second year of membership.

Because the study of student learning is so critical to the action-research process, the finding that half of these faculties developed studies tracking student learning in the first two years is noteworthy. In some cases, the analysis was only a faculty meeting spent poring over standardized test data, but, cursory or not, these faculties were trying to learn how to incorporate the study of student learning into their repertoire.

Perhaps the most striking finding was that the schools that developed a focus on student learning or curriculum and instruction were the same schools that collected data relative to student learning. The other half neither collected learning-relevant data nor developed a schoolwide student-learning focus. The remainder of this section deals with data uses by those schools that developed a student-learning-oriented focus and also collected some sort of data related to student learning.

Table 6.2 presents information about use of data other than summative standardized test results.

In their second year, the number of schools describing the collection of data other than standardized test results rose from 5 to 16. These "other" information sources included samples of student writing, numbers of books read, retention figures, formative analysis of student grades, and analysis of number and types of behavioral problems. A few schools began to study student responses to instruction.

T A B L E   6.2

NUMBER OF ORIGINAL 24 SCHOOLS CITING DATA SOURCES OTHER THAN STANDARDIZED TESTS

Dates of Action Plans

	Jan/Feb 1990 *N=24	May 1990 N=24	Feb 1991 N=21	May 1991 N=22
Schools	5	7	8	16

* N indicates the number of school action plans available for analysis.

The trend for schools entering the League later was similar—few identified sources other than the results of standardized tests for determining needs or assessing progress on their goals and/or initiatives during their first year of membership. During their second year, however, approximately two-thirds of the schools broadened the

T A B L E   6.3

NUMBER OF SCHOOLS CITING SURVEYS OF STUDENTS' RESPONSES TO OR ATTITUDES TOWARD SOCIAL, INTELLECTUAL/ACADEMIC, OR PHYSICAL EXPERIENCES OCCURRING DURING SCHOOL

Dates of Action Plans

	Jan/Feb 1990 *N=24	May 1990 N=24	Feb 1991 N=21	May 1991 N=22
Schools	5	9	10	13
**Total Citations	5	11	12	16

* N indicates the number of school action plans available for analysis.

** Some school faculties used more than one survey as part of their data-gathering process.

types of data used. About a third have not broadened the base of data collected during their several years with the League.

Table 6.3 presents the number of schools that collected information on students' experiences in school—information beyond grades or fate-control measures such as suspensions and retentions.

Surveys of student attitudes and opinions, teachers' estimates of the social climate, and parent opinion gradually entered the picture, until, by the end of the second year, about half the schools had added surveys to their data-gathering. Also, the schools using survey methods gradually moved from very general questions such as "How do you like the school?" to more specific requests for information such as "Please describe your reaction to the proposed schedule changes." Some faculty members indicated that responses to the more specific questions were more useful in making decisions and assessing the effects of actions. The trends were clearly in the direction of more data collection and more focused efforts.

How were the data used, once collected? Table 6.4 is taken from facilitator reports at the end of the second year of League operation. At that time, 21 schools were in their first year and 22 in their second year of membership. Table 6.4 summarizes data use from 35 of these 43 schools (15 schools were first-year members; 20 were second-year members).

TABLE 6.4

DATA COLLECTION, ORGANIZATION, INTERPRETATION, AND ACTION-RELATED USE BY 35 SCHOOLS AS DESCRIBED IN THE REPORTS BY FACILITATORS

Status	First-year Members	Second-year Members	Total
No data collected	5	6	11 (31%)
Data collected and organized	6	7	13 (37%)
Data analyzed and interpreted	2	4	6 (17%)
Schoolwide actions taken	2	3	5 (14%)
Total	15	20	35 (99% rounded)

The picture of data use in Table 6.4, combined with general descriptions of data use in the facilitator's reports, was of particular value to the university team. Primarily, the team realized that it was taking much longer than had been anticipated for the schools to establish a process to collect and organize data, interpret it, and take action. Eleven schools had not collected data. Thirteen had collected and organized data but were having trouble interpreting it. Several of the 13 were overwhelmed by a mass of data they had collected. Several others had realized that the information was not what they wanted; they had to collect new and different data for their purposes. Six schools had data they could interpret but had not taken any action resulting from the analysis. Five of the 35 were taking action.

The overall picture for the second-year schools was slightly better than for the first-year schools.

A similar analysis, made two years later, indicated that 25 of the 54 members at that time were making changes or taking action based on data collection and analysis. Seven were in their fourth year, 11 in their third year, and seven in their second year.

Nine of the 25 member schools reported schoolwide initiatives in the language arts. Three of those nine reported increasing writing instruction throughout their schools. Three more schools developed new courses based on needs that emerged through the analysis of data.

Of these 12 who made changes in curriculum and instruction, only two developed a system for tracking implementation or the effects on students. Changes besides curriculum and instruction made by the 25 schools varied from minor organizational adjustments to the hiring of additional personnel. Changes were made in the following areas by three to five schools:

- scheduling of courses and personnel
- communication processes within the faculty or between school and community
- staff: additions
- volunteers: increasing the number
- providing older students as tutors or mentors
- staff development: additions or revisions
- courses: adding new units or revising content
- discipline: techniques and strategies
- computer and science labs: additions and expanded use
- grading or examination policies: revisions

For the League as a whole, the picture after the fourth year was better than after the second year. Some schools were beginning to use the entire action-research paradigm. Many more were working their way through it. Several appeared to be stuck at the phase of organizing data collection. While only 12 schools made changes in curriculum and instruction or followed those changes *with regular data collection to track the effects,* the increase between 1992 and 1994 in the proportion of schools using data is an indication of progress in action research, even if the whole inquiry paradigm is not followed.

Use of "External" Information. During the orientation to the League and in subsequent meetings and conferences, the university staff urged faculties to tap the professional literature for ideas about their areas of interest. For example, if they were interested in the teaching of writing, they were urged to examine research on writing, instruments for measuring quality in writing, and so forth.

The information-retrieval system, offered as a service of the League, was designed to provide schools with external information relevant to their schoolwide goals and initiatives. Table A-5 (see Appendix) displays information on the use of the Information Retrieval System by the schools from 1990 to 1994. For 1993-94, 39 of the 54 member schools made requests for information that related to their school goals or initiatives. One hundred fifty-nine requests were made.

The six topics on which searches were requested by 15 to 20 schools each were as follows: (1) nongraded, multiage approaches; (2) site-based management; (3) at-risk students; (4) discipline; (5) alternative assessment; and (6) teacher/management/climate issues such as class size, teaching assistants, time management, scheduling, year-round schools, and teacher morale. Note again that curriculum and instruction are not among the most common areas listed.

According to the facilitators' reports at the end of the fourth year, nine schools reported studying articles and other external sources as part of their action-research process. For these nine faculties, the study of external information had permeated the culture sufficiently to be identified as a data source that informed their collective decision-making process. They consulted the professional literature when studying an area of interest, looking for methods of gathering data or planning an initiative.

Many other schools used the system to borrow articles, books, and videotapes. However, provision of information does not mean utilization, and the use of external information did not turn up in their plans.

Initiatives Made but Not Described in Relation to Data Use. As the League schools developed a shared-governance mode of operation, about half of them made initiatives to change some aspect of the operation of the school without progressing through the action-research cycle. Many of these initiatives emerged from discussions.

Imagine that some faculty members in a school begin to discuss the reading habits of students and express the opinion that students don't voluntarily read many books of their own choice. Someone suggests that they build into the day a time-slot that is earmarked for independent reading. A proposal is made and voted on and eventually the decision is made to initiate such a program. What has not been done is to collect data about the students' actual reading habits, thus clarifying the picture; to examine alternative courses of action should a problem be agreed on; and to try an initiative, collecting information about its effect on the students.

Sometimes faculties used some aspect of the action-research process in relation to an initiative that came about through a process that resembled the scenario described above. For example, they might use a survey to try to learn how the students feel about the initiative, or they might see if library circulation rose.

Summary Comments on Data Collection and Use. Few League school faculties collect data and use the results to reflect on and shape practice on a weekly, monthly, or quarterly basis. The long intervals between data points (often year-to-year or quarter-to-quarter) render many kinds of data about student achievement and behavior impossible to use in a formative fashion and mitigate the use of data to inform current practice. However, while the reflection-and-response time may be a little slow to be called "action research," the schools' use of data has changed: more League schools collect data and use the results on a year-by-year basis now than before they entered the League.

Clearly, schoolwide action research is a big, tough innovation for most faculties. What appears so straightforward in theory—scan the environment, select an area or areas to study, collect data relevant to the area(s), interpret those data, and select an action(s) designed to improve practice or performance in that area—is not easy to implement.

STUDYING EFFECTS ON STUDENTS

Because of the slow evolution of action research in most schools, it was not until the 1993-94 study that the research team focused on the schools' study of the implementation of their initiatives and indications that student learning had changed as a result. The study of the effects on students and/or student environments involved the 41 schools for whom complete data were available during that academic year.

Effects on the Learning Environment. Aside from making curricular and instructional changes, many of the schools made changes that were intended to affect the interface of the students with the schools. Fourteen schools reported making such changes: nine elementary, two middle, and three high schools. Four were fourth-year League members, five were third-year members, and five were second-year members. They reported a variety of initiatives and effects.

For example, six reported that students have more opportunities to read books of their choice during the school day. Four schools reported that their classrooms and schools operate more as a community or family, with less segregation by ability level. Three reported providing more time for students to write during the school day and more instruction in writing. Two schools reported installing new computer labs, and two schools offered new courses to their students. (Examples total more than 14 because three schools made more than one change.)

Effects on Student Participation in Schoolwide Decisions. Four elementary and five secondary schools reported increased student involvement in schoolwide issues. These nine schools reported various techniques for involving students in the decision-making process. Three high schools included a student or students on the school leadership team.

Two elementary schools and one high school formed a body of students to make recommendations. For example, one elementary school formed a student group to survey and interview students about "rules to live by" in their school. Student representatives from every kindergarten through fifth-grade classroom met with the leadership team, gathered information from classmates, organized the information and presented it to the leadership team, and continued to report back and forth between their classrooms and the leadership team until they reached agreement about common principles of community behavior.

Three other schools, two elementary and one high school, have established a pattern of roundtable and town-meeting sessions during which students are asked about specific issues, discuss concerns, or respond to questions about possible initiatives.

Effects on Student Behavior or Achievement. During the 1993-94 school year, 11 League schools (five elementary, four middle, and two high schools) reported improvements in student achievement and/or behavior based on their initiatives. Two of these schools had been members for four years, five for three, and four for two.

Five of these schools reported increases in student achievement as indicated by course grades and/or results of standardized achievement tests. In general, we do not know the magnitude of these changes, for some schools shared the results of their organized data and others did not. Five of these schools (two of these were high schools that also reduced student failure rate and improved course grades) had major reductions in referrals and suspensions. An emphasis for these schools was to have students present for instruction and to keep a sharp, collective watch on the number of referrals, suspensions, and absences. They looked at when and where incidents occurred, what was done as followup, and what seemed to work with repeat offenders.

One of the elementary schools had reduced its referral and suspension rate by approximately 25 percent each year for three years running. A middle school faculty had been effective enough through its family or "House" units and counseling program that referrals and inhouse suspensions have been cut in half. That school reported that the number of students sent to alternative school the first semester of 1992-93 was 191. For the first semester of 1993-94, the number was reduced to 81. One elementary school faculty whose initiative was to increase students' reading and writing recorded 58,284 books read outside of school by its 660 students.

Among the types of changes reported by the other schools were improvements in attendance (two schools), improvements in student self-esteem as indicated by the pre/posttest results of a student self-esteem survey and by teacher observations, and improved attitudes toward mathematics as indicated by the results of an end-of-year student survey.

Teacher Reflections on Student Effects. One of the purposes of schoolwide action research is to generate a culture where the faculties move from judgments based primarily on individual perceptions to a culture where collective analysis of data provides a reasonable degree of consensus. We are struck by how slowly this happens—how the old and comfortable perceptual worlds continue to be relied on during a process designed to build actions and understandings from common data.

Each year League facilitators have conducted interviews with a minimum of four staff members in each school. A perennial question asks about the effects of current initiatives on students. A funny thing happens repeatedly. When we ask about effects on students, the responses elicited do not describe effects on students. Instead, interviewees often describe the attributes of the current initiative (a topic that had been addressed earlier in the interview), or they describe their personal responses, or they indicate that it is too early to determine any results for students.

This phenomenon occurs even in those schools that have made initiatives clearly designed to affect students and have collected and organized data to track effects. When this response is followed by a probe about specific data (which the interviewer is familiar with), most interviewees talk about what they "feel" is happening, what they "see" happening for students, and what they "know" has changed about or for students. As Glickman would say, they respond in terms of "cardiac data," what they know in their hearts is happening, not in terms of evidence they have collected. *Only in those schools where faculties are conducting strong schoolwide action research, or struggling to do so, do interviewee responses provide a consensus about what is happening for students in their school through their collective action.*

The 1993-94 study that reported the effects on students and the number of schools that made changes or took action based on the analysis of data is informing (Calhoun and Allen 1994). As dismaying as it is to say, few schools made changes in curriculum or instruction *followed by* regular data collection to track the effects on students. Members of the League are increasing the collective use of data, but the whole inquiry paradigm that involves continual diagnosis and reflection and the study of results and possible actions has not become a way of life in many League schools.

CULTURAL DIMENSIONS AND NORMATIVE STANCES

In this section, we discuss League schools in terms of the cultural dimensions of educational change for school renewal and attempt to describe how the process of schoolwide action research interacted with school culture. Normative behavior is the focus. We move from simply reporting data from the 1992, 1993, and 1994 studies to attempt to understand why the findings occurred and how the action-research process can be improved.

The existing culture of most American schools—and most American businesses (Drucker 1985, 1989)—is not perfectly matched with the processes of schoolwide or companywide action research. To succeed, action research must change the culture of the organization. In fact, it was designed to do just that, in the same fashion that a very similar approach, Total Quality Management, was designed to do so.

A curious dilemma is built into the attempt to improve organizations by means of data-based, democratic examination of both the general health of the organization and performance in the major areas of function. The dilemma is that the *existing culture presents obstacles to the very process that would improve it.* The successful project is one that overcomes those obstacles by changing the culture. The successful project goes beyond specific innovations, though they are essential, and interrupts the circular process that has depressed innovative capability and collective, information-based efforts to improve organizations.

Thus, deeply realized, action research can make several important changes in the culture of the educational community. Conversely, until those changes are made, several aspects of the traditional culture of educational communities will impede action research. Getting action research going in the normative organizational culture requires considerable determination and energy. On balance, given the magnitude of the changes required and the very "light support" provided to help these faculties establish radically different ways of working together for educational improvement, League school faculties have done well.

DEMOCRACY IN THE FACULTY

Schoolwide action research can transform a faculty into a democratic, problem-solving group. The charter for shared governance developed by most League school faculties actually serves as a blueprint for aspects of cultural change because schools have not traditionally operated as democracies. The development of these charters for democratic behavior within the school community would not be necessary if all the precepts of the United States Constitution were being observed in every school. If our Constitution were to serve as a guideline for decision-making in schools, action research would be a much easier innovation to pursue. Thus, the League schools are trying to create an environment that reflects the deeper values of society—to create a place where people work and think together, a place that engages in continual collaborative inquiry around life and learning.

By the fourth year of League operation, much larger proportions of faculty members indicated that they were involved in decision-making that affected their work (30 of the 60 schools). About 75 percent of the teachers and paraprofessionals interviewed in these 30 schools reported that inclusion in decision-making had become a factor in their professional lives.

Teachers, and in some cases paraprofessionals and teaching assistants, are sharing in decisions through representative bodies such as school councils or leadership teams. Some of the decision-making falls within the action-research paradigm, but much does not. They make curriculum decisions, such as whether they will use textbooks in some courses, whether they will adopt "whole language," whether they will develop thematic units. They make decisions about the organization of education for students and how opportunities will be provided, such as how to integrate all student populations more fully into the regular classroom, how to engage "turned-off" students, and how to develop technological expertise among their students. They are involved in decisions about whether to have telephones in the teachers' lounge, the length of time between class periods, and the operation of in-school-suspension systems.

Literally hundreds of decisions have been made by the League faculties working as a unit over the last half-dozen years. Many of those that are not made within the action-research paradigm are well within the definitions of school improvement that are used by many of the current "restructuring" strategies in the field of education.

The focus here, however, is on the use of the action-research process on a schoolwide basis and the development of a democratic, data-oriented culture within which action research is a routine way of doing business.

The struggle to replace nondemocratic norms in the League schools is evident in the data discussed throughout this chapter. Schools put a toe in the water and gradually increase areas open to collective action. Getting into student learning, curriculum, and instruction takes great energy and strong leadership until studying those areas becomes a comfortable routine in the life of a faculty.

The less democratic the school is before the action-research process starts, the more difficult will be the change process and the more resistance will be generated. The process is much more complex than working out a procedure that brings things to a vote or results in a consensus wherein principal and faculty share a decision.

The decisions need to be informed ones where information has been collected and discussed widely; the whole communication system has to change.

Communication about schoolwide changes and the rationale for these changes has improved in about three-fifths of the League schools. In 30 schools (25 of these were among the 30 schools that indicated broader involvement in their schoolwide decision-making process), the data indicate that staff members are more informed about what is happening in their schools and that information-sharing and reflection about practice have increased.

Gradually, schools have added more structures for communicating information within the faculties, and in some cases have developed more ways of communicating to parents and the public. In some schools, leadership teams have learned to disseminate minutes of their meetings to the rest of the faculty—a small task, but the addition reflects a growing recognition of the importance of communication. Most schools have developed liaison or study groups that provide a two-way flow of information between facilitation teams and other staff members. Interviews with principals and teachers indicated that principals are working harder at communicating a broader range of information than was true earlier. And the increased amount and depth of communication were spoken of favorably in most interviews.

In terms of Rosenholtz' (1989) useful distinction between "moving" and "stuck" schools, it appears that between two-thirds and three-fourths of the League schools are making a transition into the "moving" state with respect to the development of democratic processes for communicating and making decisions. The others appear to be battling, somewhat unsuccessfully, against the homeostatic forces ingrained in the traditional culture of schooling.

THE INVOLVEMENT OF STUDENTS IN COLLECTIVE INQUIRY

Within the League framework, we encourage school faculties moving into shared governance to focus first on sharing decisions between teachers and administrators, and to include other members of the community such as paraprofessionals, students, parents, and community members as they wish. In schoolwide action research, we encourage school faculties to involve students from the beginning: inform students of the goals or involve them in identifying schoolwide goals; involve them in collecting data, and, when possible, in organizing, analyzing, and interpreting these data; update them in terms of progress; and involve them in identifying possible actions to be tested through implementation.

While we know that student learning goals cannot be attained without student participation, the movement toward viewing students as participating members rather than as subjects remains slow. Only nine of the schools have found some way of increasing student participation.

TIME TO MEET AND THINK TOGETHER

The daily and weekly schedules of most schools provide very little time for meetings, discussions, and study, making it extremely difficult to establish the school as a center for collective inquiry. Lack of time to work together is cited regularly as a major impediment to progress (Calhoun 1992, Calhoun and Glickman 1993). People need time to organize and study the data they collect, to read and discuss external information, and to discuss the results of current actions and formulate future actions.

We recommend that about one-half day per week be set aside for faculty study, decision-making, and staff development. That may sound like a drastic change in schedule and it is. However, the effect on the school culture can be profound, and we regard it as essential. The League schools that made the most progress made some kind of headway with the time problem, developing a structure that permits discussion, data analysis, and decision-making to be richer and less forced than in those schools that are trying to generate schoolwide action research within the time allocations that have been traditional in our schools.

THE PLACE OF DATA IN THE ENVIRONMENT

Making the decision process not only collective but founded on data is a real cultural change. School faculties that rarely use schoolwide data on a regular basis remain stuck in the summative, judgmental use of data instead of moving into the formative use of data to guide current decisions and practices. The "stuck" League schools study no data as a faculty or they collect data and use them on a year-by-year basis rather than on a weekly, monthly, or quarterly basis. These long intervals between data points render many kinds of data about student achievement and behavior impossible to use in a formative fashion and mitigate the use of data to inform current practice.

We know that effective cycles of data use and reflection are not present in the culture of most contemporary U.S. schools (Goodlad 1984, Sirotnik 1987). The patterns of behavior needed to sustain this collective study are foreign to current cultural patterns. League faculties work hard, but the terrain is tough for most.

Schools conducting action research need to examine regularly the data that have strong consequences for the "fate" of their students. Grades are an example of what we call "fate control" data. As long as schools are assigning grades, and student progress through the organization and admittance into other educational institutions is controlled by grades, all members of each educational unit need to have some idea of how well students are progressing as indicated by these grades. But looking at those data that are so important to student life and success in school and beyond is currently an uncharacteristic practice in most schools.

Schools interested in student achievement, student motivation, and school climate need to look regularly at their referral, suspension, and absence data. One reason is that these data indicate whether students are present for instruction. There are not many "climate" indicators more powerful than whether the body is present and on time for instruction. These schools have come a long way from, in some instances, no one looking at schoolwide data, from only the chief administrator looking at data on what all students were experiencing, or from the faculty looking at the results of standardized tests to set state- or district-required "improvement goals." Gradually, more faculty members in League schools are becoming informed about what all students are experiencing. And more teachers are beginning to see, to use their own words, "the big picture."

THE RELATIONSHIP TO IDEAS AND INFORMATION GENERATED ELSEWHERE

The League as an organization hopes that data from the literature will eventually flow regularly into the decision-making process of the school.

However, as noted earlier, the collective study of external information to inform decision-making has been difficult to integrate with the norms of interaction within the schools. Only limited progress has been made in facilitating faculty use of external research or information about teaching and learning.

However, when it comes to the selection of goals and initiatives to pursue, leadership teams and faculties that do use external sources tend to adopt approaches they find, not as ideas to be tested, but as "completed" innovations that only have to be put in place to solve problems.

The contrast is between an uncritical acceptance of popular, "well-advertised" ideas and innovations and the use of externally developed ideas as springboards for serious inquiry. It is ironic that many of us seem, on one hand, not to value research enough to make it part of our decision-making process while, on the other hand, we will adopt external innovations without question. Again, we can see an aspect of the cultural change necessary if the spirit of action research is to flourish. Collective inquiry is a cultural innovation.

PROLIFERATING INITIATIVES

School district central-office staffs are often criticized for their habit of bombarding schools with an excess of initiatives—too many to support effectively—and creating a feeling of futility as little implementation occurs.

However, faculties have the same tendency—generating so many goals and initiatives that none has a significant effect on student learning or on the organization. Some schools, having identified a large number of areas to study, divide the labor in such a way that small groups develop actions but the faculty as a whole doesn't. Thus, proliferation makes it difficult to have a focus for collegial action; there are so many simultaneous demands that collective action becomes almost impossible.

League school faculties have this same tendency to attempt so much that successful attainment of their goals becomes almost impossible. League staff members have advised that initiatives should be few (one or two), be schoolwide, and be done well, but many faculties find this advice difficult to heed. At the end of the fourth year, there were 47 schools for which we believe we have reliable data about the number of initiatives that were operating. Eight were working on seven or more initiatives, 13 on five or six, and 11 on three or four.

The proliferation of initiatives and inability to focus together on a few highly valued goals at a time may be a product of a collision between the action-research paradigm and the prevailing norms of autonomy. Many teachers make suggestions for initiatives that are tailored to their situations and perceptions rather than the needs of the school as a whole. To satisfy them, those suggestions are accepted.

Before anyone realizes it, the energy for innovation has been sponged up by many small initiatives and no energy is "left over" for a collective movement.

BUILDING STAFF DEVELOPMENT INTO THE CULTURE

Some League school faculties have moved successfully through Phases 1 through 5 of the action-research process and selected or developed innovations that have great promise for improving student learning.

Now they need to implement the initiatives, which means learning new skills. Watching what happens next has a poignant side. Most know little about the knowledge base relative to how to bring about the implementation of curricular or instructional changes (Fullan and Pomfret 1977, Hall and Loucks 1977, Hall and Hord 1987, Levine 1991, Sparks and Loucks-Horsley 1992, Joyce and Showers 1995). And those who do have the knowledge have little idea about how to integrate it into their actions. Essentially, *lack of awareness of the need for and how to provide for adequate staff development to support implementation prohibits many of these faculties from attaining their collective goal(s).* Lewin reminded us in 1946 that "we should consider action, research, and training as a triangle that should be kept together for the sake of any of its corners" (p. 211).

Bluntly, if school faculties knew how to improve student learning in a particular area throughout the school, they would already be doing it. A need worth pursuing almost always requires new learning, and that new learning is probably complex curricular and instructional behavior. For most people, learning complex conceptual and behavioral tasks requires effort and instruction (Gagne 1965). Learning new teaching strategies, new ways of interacting with students, and new ways of managing time in the classroom requires staff development (Joyce and Showers 1995).

A few League school teams and faculties recognize this need, but, overall, the schools are so ingrained in current practices and attending to immediate needs that few faculties are able to generate the levels of staff development to make it possible for them to employ the innovations they select. And, even in those schools where some staff members are knowledgeable about implementation, these staff members are often overwhelmed by the "proliferation problem," for the majority of the faculty support the "smorgasbord approach" to staff development.

REFLECTIONS ON SCHOOLWIDE ACTION RESEARCH, INNOVATION, AND CULTURAL CHANGE

During their League membership, nearly all the schools have generated initiatives for school improvement—far more than most schools do in the same periods. However, relatively few of the initiatives they made required the faculties to learn new approaches to curriculum and instruction. Is it possible that staff development to learn new approaches to teaching is a larger cultural change than is innovation as such, so that schools have a tendency to confine their innovative vision to areas that will not require collective staff development?

Also, is it possible that engaging in the kind of data-based innovation that is embedded in the action-research paradigm is a larger innovation, one that challenges the school culture more, than is the substance of innovation itself? If so, we may be closer to understanding why technical assistance is of such importance, helping schools "get over the hump" of learning to inquire together and keeping their sights firmly on the curricular and instructional changes that will make the greatest difference to students.

IMPROVING THE PROCESS OF ACTION RESEARCH

During the last three years, we have engaged in two studies designed to capitalize on the experience of the League in such a way as to improve the action-research process. In the first study, we capitalized on the apparent technical-assistance needs of the League schools and provided extensive technical assistance to 11 schools in University Town, studying the effects on the progress of those schools (see chapter 3). The second study concentrated on three schools in the League and two schools in University Town that made the most progress in following the action-research paradigm.

THE UNIVERSITY TOWN STUDY OF ACTION RESEARCH

The organizational setting is described in chapter 3. Particularly relevant is the provision of time for study on a weekly basis. Although action research had to share time with district initiatives, each faculty met weekly as a whole to share data and research, discuss issues, make decisions, and study consequences.

The current study was inaugurated after it became apparent after a year of school-based action research that virtually no progress was being made despite the time available, a network of facilitators (teachers) in each school, and some technical assistance. A consultant was brought in for about 25 days during the second year; a district coordinating team was organized; teachers were organized into formal study teams; facilitators were trained in group processing and decision-making approaches and in the phases of the action-research cycle. Most of the service of the consultant was provided to the school-based and district facilitators, though on occasion service was provided directly to the faculties of individual schools.

Here are examples of the progress made during the second year:

1. In all 11 schools, collaborative decision-making and feelings of collegiality increased. Teachers and administrators reported that communication patterns had improved and that data were shared frequently. However, few students or parents were involved.

2. In their deliberations, all 11 school faculties maintained a focus on student learning. Ten collected and shared data on all students with respect to aspects of student learning, behavior, or attitudes.

3. Nine of the faculties studied the professional literature as part of their inquiry.

4. Nine made changes stemming from their data collection and analysis.

5. Nine documented that they had made changes in the learning environments of their students.

6. Five documented that the changes in learning environment had affected student achievement.

Altogether, the University Town experience supported the hypothesis that increased technical assistance would ease the passage of the schools into an action-research modality. In general, these schools followed the action-research modality with greater ease and greater success than had been the case in the previous studies. Importantly, the technical assistance had included the arrangements for time to meet and study, the provision of direct access to the literature, the organization of the faculty into study groups, the mode of working with district facilitators who, in turn, worked with school facilitators and faculties, and a number of smaller but also useful organizational arrangements.

A community was built to tend the action-research process, and that community was provided with the organizational, communication, and technical means to nurture the process. As reported in chapter 4, a consequence was that the teachers overwhelmingly supported the value of action research and urged its continuation.

STUDIES OF THE MOST SUCCESSFUL SCHOOLS: LEADERSHIP EMERGES AS A CRITICAL FACTOR

Between April 1994 and March 1995, we focused our study of action research around five of the 70 schools in the League and University Town that have made the most progress in using schoolwide action research to pursue their goals. Three of these schools are members of the League of Professional Schools and two are members of University Town.

What have we learned about action research from analyzing interviews with members of these five faculties?

A Leader Who Involves Others. Someone provides strong, visible leadership for the action-research process. Initially, the leader is only one person, an administrator or a teacher, who believes that the study of data about what students are experiencing and the use of the results to determine actions and assess progress are of value. Initially, this person may know very little about conducting action research, but he or she is willing to learn and make it a priority.

During the first year or two, this person may do much of the work of finding and developing measures to assess progress, organizing the results, presenting the information, seeking external information, and "nudging" everyone along. While this leader is doing the basic work of action research, she is also bringing a few staff members into the process either conceptually through constant dialogue about what they are doing and/or technically through involving them in tasks such as the organization of data or presentation of results. These individuals form a partnership with one or two colleagues, then gradually develop a core group—generally members of this core group came first from the school leadership/facilitator team—who work to learn the action-research process and help others understand and use it.

In the most successful schools, the members who form this core group talk about the school as if it were a giant classroom. They talk about "the big picture" of what students are experiencing and they talk about changes in their perspective from being primarily concerned about their individual classroom to being concerned about improving education in the school as a whole.

Most members of the core group tend to be long-time seekers and users of staff development and professional development opportunities as individuals. Individually and collectively, they project and articulate a sense of moral responsibility about the education of all students entrusted to their school, a professional obligation to improve practice throughout the school, and a poignant awareness of how other faculty members feel about current and proposed changes. Their leadership role and the work done by members of the core group tend to strengthen their belief in collective inquiry for school improvement.

Effective Use of Time. It is not just a matter of providing time for collective study; it's also how this time is used. The most successful faculties have time to work together regularly, use the time to analyze and interpret their data, study promising curricular and instructional practices, plan lessons and units and other collective actions together, and share their experiences and reflections about what happened.

A Facilitative Principal. The principal serves as steward of the action-research process. These principals are active participants. They serve as a full member or ex-officio member of the core group. They use organizational position, their greater mobility within the building, and their broader access to information to facilitate resources and events, such as staff development, technical assistance, more time to work on tasks, or simply greater allocations of paper.

During their work with the facilitation team or core group, these principals often ask questions not thought of by other staff members, questions that seem to come from broader experience beyond the classroom and in dealing with various special-interest groups. They play devil's advocate in relation to suggested actions or lack of action. And they tend as individuals to have more perseverance and a stronger belief that problems can be solved than do other members of the group.

Principals frequently serve as cheerleaders to the core group or facilitation team, even when they are personally frustrated by the lack of progress being made. These principals tend to radiate a combination of (1) support for the work of the group and the faculty and (2) pressure to improve education for all students.

In the most successful schools, principals use their organizational position and their interactions with the staff to keep the focus on improving student learning through curriculum and instruction. They communicate their beliefs about student learning and their commitment to schoolwide educational improvement continually. Whatever the schoolwide focus is, these principals are talking to individual teachers, paraprofessionals, parents, and students about it; asking questions about it; and often, in the case of instructional strategies that have been selected for implementation, participating in staff development, planning lessons, teaching in the classroom, and sharing their experiences along with the staff. They communicate fiercely and model the technical and social aspects of collective inquiry.

Shared Decision-Making. Almost all the schools in the League have established procedures for sharing decisions between teachers and administrators and among the faculty as a collective body. What distinguishes the more successful schools from the less successful ones in using action research to pursue common goals and change the culture of their school is (1) the breadth and depth of participation in the decision-making process, and (2) the use of the shared decision-making system to take actions over the substantive issues of teaching and learning (instruction and curriculum).

In the most successful schools, the leadership team or core group works zealously to ensure that all faculty members become informed decision-makers: they design the work of action research so that everyone engages in data collection and interpretation, studies what is working/has worked in other settings, and helps in selecting or designing actions for implementation. And while not easy for individuals as leaders or the faculty as a group, these schools tend to use their decision-making system to address curricular and instructional issues. Teacher leaders in these schools seem to become more and more passionate about including all staff members in the decision-making process, about the responsibility of the individual to be an informed community member, and about engaging in collective work around substantive issues that the staff can modify to influence student learning.

Solicitation of Outside Support. These schools secure external support for their school-improvement efforts, especially from their district office. Someone in these schools knows how to garner additional resources and support from the district office and other agencies external to the district. Initially, this person is generally the principal, though as time passes a few other staff members also become skilled in locating additional resources and exploiting—for collective study by faculty members—initiatives that are sponsored by the district and agencies external to the district.

The most successful schools go beyond requesting additional funding and rule variance. They *use* the district office staff and all their connections: they ask them to help solve problems, to provide or locate technical assistance, to provide or make provisions for staff development, to help with planning tasks, to provide additional information for the faculty to study, even to come in and help with group processing when the social difficulty of the task moves beyond the skills of the leadership team.

REFLECTIONS AND CURRENT ADVICE

We know that student effects are a difficult bottom line in school improvement (David and Peterson 1984, Louis and Miles 1990, Muncey and McQuillan 1993). We know that cultural change is difficult for our schools (Bennis 1989, Berman and Gjelten 1983, Deal 1993, Mutchler and Duttweiler 1990, Prestine 1992, Rollow and Bryk 1993, Sarason 1982 and 1990, Smith 1993, and Stigelbauer and Anderson 1992). We know that time is a longstanding problem (Goodlad 1984, David 1991, Wallace and Wildy 1993); that overload of initiatives is common (Fullan 1982, 1992, and 1993); that conscientious use of external information by the school as community is rare (Havelock and others 1969, Huberman and Miles 1984); that the lack of adequate staff development to support organizational goals is common (Joyce and Showers 1995, Levine 1991, Lezotte [see Sparks' interview] 1993); that the participation of students as members of the critical study process is complex (Butler-Kisber 1993, Strike 1993); and that the use of data to inform practice is a major cultural change (Corey 1953, Lewin 1948, Goodlad 1984, Sirotnik 1987, Miles 1992).

Yet, with all the known complexities and difficulties, courageous and determined school faculties and districts do make these changes. Each year that the work of League school faculties has been studied, collective movement forward has been witnessed in one of more of these areas (Calhoun 1991; Hensley, Calhoun, and Glickman 1992; Calhoun and Glickman 1993; Calhoun and Allen 1994).

The journey toward continuous, collective inquiry that League schools are undertaking and the successes and difficulties they encounter are the same for the League as an organization as for the schools themselves. League staff and associates are as culture-bound as school faculties are, and it is as difficult for us to change how we behave individually and collectively as it is for our school-based colleagues. We *are* of the same culture.

Allocating time for collaborative inquiry and discourse, providing time for cooperative, disciplined inquiry around the goals of the organization, providing staff development for ourselves as learners, and using continual inquiry and exploration as well as personal knowledge as we make decisions and take action are the same normative patterns we have difficulty establishing for ourselves. But, like the schools, we do not lose heart, for our quest for greater understanding and our journey toward improving educational practice through collective study and action allow us to live our belief that things can be better than they are for students of all ages.

We provide the following recommendations to faculties seeking to function as democratic, problem-solving communities:

1. Seek and work with policy-makers to ensure time for collaborative work.

2. Use an inquiry mode for learning to conduct schoolwide action research; one does not have to be "ready" or all-knowing to begin the journey or to make progress on it.

3. Develop and tend a core group to lead the effort, with the chief administrator as a working member of this group.

4. Keep the focus on student learning.

5. Provide for staff development and capability-building as a regular component, rather than making *ad hoc* arrangements for specific innovations.

Deal (1993) reminds us that the same shared culture that gives meaning and stability to the process of education also "frustrates efforts to improve, reform, or change educational forms and practices at all levels." The changes that many of us want for ourselves and our students as a part of schoolwide action research will alter the existing culture of our classrooms and schools. Consequently, serious action research is tough work in most school settings. Too often, our stance as we engage in it becomes one of activity accomplishment instead of inquiry, one of moving through the steps instead of exploration of effects. When this occurs, we have little cultural change. Schoolwide action research simply dissolves into the stable culture as have many other promising innovations in education. We must *will it and live it;* otherwise we and our schools will remain the same, and we will have only tinkered with the edges of our potential and the potential educational world of our students.

CHAPTER 7

SCHOOL RENEWAL: AN INQUIRY, NOT A PRESCRIPTION

BRUCE JOYCE AND EMILY CALHOUN

Where are we in our inquiry? We close with a brief review of our interpretations of the experiences of the five programs. Then we share the hypotheses that we are pursuing as we develop other programs and studies.

INTERPRETATIONS

Throughout the case studies, we have reported data and observations and reflected on them, trying to increase our own knowledge-in-practice. Looking back, several results from one or more of the cases have particular relevance to the design of staff development and school-renewal programs.

ON INVOLVEMENT

All five cases illustrated that not only can school renewal involve all the teachers in a school right from the beginning of a program, but faculties as a whole can be involved in district renewal. River City, University Town, and Readersville all involved *everybody* and succeeded in developing very high degrees of implementation and student effects. Further, simultaneous initiatives are possible, up to a point, provided adequate staff development is included. University Town was particularly effective. However, a proliferation of initiatives is lethal, as many of the Action Network schools have found. Leagues of schools working together can function well, but only with large amounts of technical assistance, including extensive onsite service.

These messages are important, because many program planners have believed that whole-school or whole-district efforts would fall prey to massive resistance. Thus, many planners have begun with small groups of volunteers, or "leaders," or they have created numerous "small-group" collaboratives within a school; none of these piecemeal strategies has been very effective for improving student learning schoolwide. In these five programs, there were enormous advantages because of the extensive involvement of all personnel from the outset.

ON GOVERNANCE

District, school, and individual initiatives all generated considerable satisfaction in University Town, but all needed careful tending. In Action Network, we can see very clearly the struggle to establish democracy in the face of the individualistic normative traditions of schools. Collaborative governance is foreign territory for many schools and districts. Even after years of working together and experiencing great success in improving student learning, many faculties have difficulty making collective decisions and taking coordinated action.

Highly skilled leadership, expert technical assistance, and ample social support appear necessary to establish democracy-in-action, even in settings where it is strongly encouraged and supported by teacher and administrator leadership activity and financial resources.

ON THE CHARACTERISTICS OF TEACHERS AND ADMINISTRATORS

In University Town and River City, neither age nor experience— subjects of intense study—had an effect on teachers' or administrators' ability to learn, support for initiatives, or enthusiasm for collaborative governance. However, "states of growth" of individuals were a factor in implementation, affirmation of initiatives, and leadership ability. Again, a substantial number of program planners in the past have assumed that age was a negative factor. On the contrary, seasoned lead teachers played critical roles in all the programs.

ON STUDENT LEARNING

Substantive initiatives in teaching/curriculum resulted in significant increases in student learning in River City, University Town, Readersville, and Inner City. In some cases, the increases in student achievement were *several times* greater than the rates of learning that were found in baseline studies.

Implementation was a powerful factor influencing student achievement. The clearest evidence was in River City, where, at the extreme, an effect size of 2.0 appeared between the classes of the most and least skilled uppergrade teachers. In the other settings, implementation had similar effects, including Action Network, where the schools that implemented the entire action-research paradigm made documented gains, but schools that achieved only partial implementation made little or "unknown" progress with student learning or with assessing the effects of their actions.

Many program planners have assumed that student-achievement effects will take years. Not so in these programs or in several others, such as Success for All, the Pittsburgh Program, Distar, or the best of the Mastery Learning implementations. We theorize that the innovations that will make a difference in student achievement will do so in the first year of implementation—the second at the latest. Children respond to improved learning environments *right away.*

ON CADRE DEVELOPMENT: TEACHERS AS TEACHER TRAINERS

In River City, a cadre of teachers was able to support 16 schools. Seven of these schools were studied with respect to student achievement, as measured by the Iowa Tests of Basic Skills, and implementation reached the point where gains in student learning were substantial. In University Town, another cadre is carrying the primary responsibility of staff development and training as this is written. In other settings, Just Read is being demonstrated and supported in new schools by teacher leaders.

In the past, cadres of teachers have been seriously underutilized in many settings.

ON TECHNICAL ASSISTANCE

Technical assistance from external colleagues was available in all five programs. It was most extensive in River City and Inner City, extensive in University Town, less extensive in Readersville, and lightest in Action Network. Internal technical assistance—from central-office personnel, principals, and teacher leaders—was most extensive and had the greatest breadth of involvement in University Town and Readersville, as districtwide innovations were implemented and sustained.

As they seek to change the status quo in their school or district, most faculties need conceptual and social colleagueship from outside their organization. For capability-building and social support for the changes they seek to make, most school and district faculties need internal technical assistance. Provisions for this technical assistance need to be structured into the school-renewal program, not be the result of happenstance or the response to a crisis. Provisions for internal support designed into these five programs include time to meet as a faculty (structure) and study groups, cadre, and facilitation teams (groups).

THE SOCIAL DIMENSION

The social cohesion of faculties affected implementation in all settings.

Quality of leadership by central-office personnel, principals, and teachers varied and generated variance in implementation. Regardless of role or position, successful leadership in school renewal requires the effort to expand one's technical and social repertoire. Teachers and administrators who try to stay within their current repertoire can become upset if that repertoire proves inadequate. Teachers and administrators who are expanding their knowledge and skills and are comfortable with inquiry as a way of life obtain great satisfaction from school-renewal efforts.

DIRECTIONS IN SCHOOL IMPROVEMENT

Conceptually, school improvement is evolving in a direction away from relatively compact, focused innovations intended to solve specific educational problems, and toward a fluid, continuous inquiry into how to make education better on a day-to-day basis. The intent is to make all schools learning communities for faculties as well as students—making use of the most powerful models of learning with both groups.

For schools to become learning communities, however, significant organizational changes are required. For many years and through many different reform movements, our schools have been hampered by structural characteristics that make innovation laborious: no embedded time in the workday for collegial inquiry, no structures for democratic decision-making, the absence of a fluid information-rich environment, and the absence of a pervasive staff development system. Essentially, we have tried to engage in school improvement with a series of Catch-22s designed into our organization.

Consequently, our school-improvement efforts have primarily used those limited and ineffective strategies that can live within inhospitable conditions for change. When a problem area has been identified by a faculty—for example, "modernize the science curriculum," "help 'at-risk' students," "teach more students to read effectively," "tend the 'gifted and talented'," "provide for 'Limited English Proficiency' students"—the usual solution has been to find a procedure that could be administered without the benefits of a problem-solving, learning community. Thus, special programs were generated for nearly every category of student and grafted onto the school, staffed separately with new cadres of specialists. New curriculums were designed and "put in place," euphemistically speaking, with limited amounts of training or involvement by the teachers in deciding how to make them work.

Recognizing the limited successes of those tactics, reformers have assigned responsibility for improving the schools to the faculties, newly empowered by school-based budgeting to spend discretionary money for staff development and school improvement. Yet, without the structural and procedural changes that provide for continuous, collective inquiry, faculties have labored to pick up the challenge, and the odds have been against them.

What is now envisioned is a quantum leap toward the creation of a setting where inquiry is normal and the conditions of the workplace support the continuous, collegial inquiry that treats innovations as opportunities to study. The vision is of a "School as a Center of Inquiry" (Schaefer 1967), where teaching and learning are examined continuously and improved in the course of engagement, and where students are brought into the world of studying not only what they are learning in the curricular sense, but also into studying their own capability as learners.

Hence, the terms *constructivism* and *metacognition* come into the vocabulary of school renewal, pulling teaching toward the processes of helping students develop knowledge and study themselves as learners and pulling school improvement toward the processes of helping individual teachers and faculties develop knowledge and study themselves and their environment.

We believe a different culture of education will result. Relationships among teachers, between teachers and students, between teachers and administrators, and between educators and laymen will change. "Solutions" and school-improvement plans will be formulated as hypotheses to be tested, rather than as panaceas that, once in place, solve the problem. Democracy will replace bureaucracy; collaboration will replace isolation; faculties working as a community of professionals seeking knowledge and applying its results as hypotheses will replace the small group of courageous educators in every school who have accepted the responsibility of seeking and promoting the latest approach to school improvement.

This evolution changes our professional life from solitary inquiry to collective inquiry, while at the same time supporting individual flexibility and development. The goal for school renewal is for everyone—working together and alone—to become more capable.

RECREATING THE SCHOOL THROUGH INQUIRY

School renewal as inquiry is a quiet revolution. Rather than being a campaign to replace one set of educational practices with another, school renewal seeks to recreate the organization so that specific initiatives emanate from within that organization.

What are the essential elements of this organizational reconstruction? The focus is on the school's capacity to improve the learning capability of the students and the faculty. The process is one of school-based inquiry, involves the total faculty, builds community, serves to increase student learning through the study of instruction and curriculum, and seeks to provide a nurturant organization through collective study of the health of the school.

All this sounds familiar enough, doesn't it—a reprise of the trends of the times? But, although the words are familiar, the composition of the tune is somewhat different and is partly, though not entirely, a matter of boldness and emphasis.

But just how does a faculty (of a district, as well as a school) get started? Many of us have a sense of what our work environment needs to become a healthier learning place, but where do we go from here and how do we get there? How can schools increase capability? We suggest that faculties explore promising changes and test them as hypotheses, finding out whether they do, indeed, change the learning community.

The following six hypotheses are grounded to some degree in research, such as the case studies we have reported in this book, and they capture the elements common to reportedly successful school-improvement programs. However, we believe they need to be tested anew in each setting. Actions based on them need to be adapted and modified as evidence is gathered to assess them.

HYPOTHESIS 1:

RESTRUCTURING JOB ASSIGNMENTS AND SCHEDULES TO BUILD TIME FOR COLLECTIVE INQUIRY INTO THE WORKPLACE WILL INCREASE SCHOOL-IMPROVEMENT ACTIVITY.

From isolation to synergy: Restructuring time. Our first hypothesis pertains to creating time for collective adult interaction. The building in of time during the workday for collegial process *as an entire faculty* is central to school renewal. Some school-improvement strategies assume that the schedule of the school will remain the same, but schoolwide change requires time for all members of the organization to work and study together. Without this collective study time, we cannot move forward as a learning community, only as individual "points of light."

Synergistic environments—environments characterized by rigorous interchange among people—foster inquiry. Environments that separate people depress inquiry. Our schools were not designed as synergistic environments. They were designed for the adults who work within their walls to function separately, rather than for those adults to engage in professional inquiry and support. Schools' organizational structures make it difficult for colleagueship to flourish, and their design suppresses synergy.

Many of us have worked in schools that were and still are organized as a loose federation of little schools (classrooms) with the minimum of adult interchange built into the workplace—an almost absolute minimum needed to keep the place operating. Our school year began with one or two days of meetings to get regulations clear and to get our assignments to instructional spaces and duties. Often, we were brought together as a faculty for just a few hours before we fanned out into our classrooms. Some of us taught without really knowing our colleagues down the hall or even what our neighbor "next door" was doing.

In such a structure, the making of curriculum, the creation of a nurturant social climate, the collective study of students and what they are learning, and the study of the health of the organization as a unit are nearly impossible. As we examine the history of school-reform movements, we are amazed that teachers and administrators have been able to keep the school as healthy as it is. School improvement has been inherently frustrating simply because time to study has not been part of our job. We need each other and we need time to work together. We need each other's ideas for stimulation, and we need each other's perspectives to enrich our own perceptions.

Brief Scenario: Example of a Schedule Change. In the Pala Elementary and High School District, the students leave after lunch every Wednesday afternoon. From 1:30 p.m. until 4:00 p.m. every Wednesday, the faculties in this district meet to develop and tend the learning community.

In this district the assignment had been "Here's your classroom and here's the list of students assigned to you." Now the assignment is "Welcome to a learning community where teaching and learning are studied as they are carried on." And *time* to do so is embedded into the work week. Will embedded time for professional interchange enhance the schooling process for the Pala District? We think so, and faculties there are testing the idea.

HYPOTHESIS 2:

ACTIVE DEMOCRACY AND COLLECTIVE INQUIRY, WITH FACULTY AND COMMUNITY MEMBERS WORKING TOGETHER, CREATE THE STRUCTURAL CONDITIONS IN WHICH THE PROCESS OF SCHOOL IMPROVEMENT IS NESTED.

The traditional managerial structure for our schools and school districts has been a loose federation of classrooms somewhat coordinated by principals and their assistants and a few central-office personnel responsible for general administration and support. Our classrooms are loosely connected to one another and to the school administration, and our schools are loosely connected to district management structures (Baldridge and Deal 1983, Murphy and Hallinger 1993, Weick 1976).

State departments of education are on the periphery and often serve local districts and schools much like financial backers with guidelines and standards for the use of public resources. Most state departments have virtually no structure other than curriculum frameworks and standards for communicating their educational intents or for supporting the implementation of these intents.

Thus, as it has been and probably should continue to be, those closest to the student—the school community and its faculty—carry the educational system. So, how do we "manage ourselves" in a more effective fashion? We have several hierarchical divisions (schools, districts, and state departments) managing their aspects of the educational system, often using compliance with regulations instead of integrated cognitions about student learning and school improvement as stimulants for change. What "managerial transformation" can all divisions support that can be done right now to help those closest to the education of the student—the school community and its faculty?

Building a Democratic Community: The Responsible Parties. We suggest the formation of a democratic governing body for each school (Glickman 1993) with parents and other community members included in the process. This group will function as "Responsible Parties" for the health of the school. In a small school, let us include all faculty members on the governing body. In a larger school, let us elect representatives. And in both small schools and large, the community elects representatives.

Rather than being a traditional parliamentary governing group, our Responsible Parties will be an inquiring group, leading all members of the community in the study of the school, of the students, and of ways of making the school and the education it offers continually better. Decision-making roles, leadership roles, and responsibility are all expanded. Major decisions are made with the participation of all faculty members, along with elected representatives from the community, and with administrators functioning as the "executive secretaries" of the governing body.

Brief Scenario: Example of a Responsible Democratic Community. Rincon Elementary School has 18 teachers and 500 students. The Responsible Parties include all 18 teachers, 18 parents elected by the other parents, and four student-parent teams.

Rincon High School has 66 teachers and 1,600 students. A building leadership team of 16 teachers and 16 parents are on the Responsible Parties team, along with four student-parent teams.

In neither case are the Responsible Parties legislative units, since all teachers and parents vote on important decisions. However, in both cases the Responsible Parties lead the development of the learning community, tend it, ensure that the democratic inquiry process is supported at the individual and school level, and coordinate initiatives within the school.

At Rincon, professionals and laymen work together with the benefit of the children as the goal that binds them and inquiry as the process that unifies them for collective action. Every practice in the school is open for inquiry rather than being considered as a permanent solution. If something isn't working for a child or a group of children, the failure is acknowledged and something else tried, without blame or shame, but in the full realization that teaching is a never-ending process of trying to reach all the kids in the best ways that current vision permits.

HYPOTHESIS 3:
LEARNING TO STUDY THE LEARNING ENVIRONMENT WILL INCREASE INQUIRY INTO WAYS OF HELPING STUDENTS LEARN BETTER.

Inquiry involves the collection and analysis of data and reflection on them. In an odd sense, our schools have been both information-rich and information-impoverished. The richness lies in the prodigious information-gathering that goes on in schools. Teachers teach, test, and assess the results. However, schools have lacked the reflective, experimental qualities whereby assessment of learning leads to the study of ways of improving it.

In a River City middle school, only 30 percent of the students earned promotion at the end of each school year. All the teachers had information indicating that their students were failing to learn the prescribed material in their courses. Year after year, they knew the students were failing. And yet, year after year, the students failed. The faculty never met as a community to reflect on the failure rate or to study what was happening. Then, a staff development program interrupted the situation by bringing the faculty into the study of teaching. Students began to learn more, and within two years, 95 per cent of them were earning promotion with the same curriculum and the same tests still in place.

What happened in this middle school? Faculty members, working as an organizational unit, began to study the learner and the learning environment they were providing. Data about student learning came to be used differently—as information sources for the faculty to analyze as they inquired into how their students could become more powerful learners. Information that had existed in the school for years came to have meaning and utility as it was studied by these faculty members (Joyce, Murphy, Showers, and Murphy 1989).

Every school has large quantities of data available as a resource for collective inquiry. These data sources can be used to inform us about obvious problems, such as low achievement; they also can be used to examine all aspects of the school environment and what students are experiencing as members of this environment.

For example, let's move away from the example of the low-achieving middle school to look at some schools with a history of high achievement (University Town). These schools have students who are acknowledged to be very high achieving (in achievement the district ranked in the top 5 percent of the nation's schools on standard tests). Elementary faculties in this district inquired into the quality of student writing and into the teaching of writing, and within two years, the quality of student writing had improved several times beyond its predicted rate based on previous years' growth (Joyce, Calhoun, Carran, Halliburton, Rust, and Simser 1994).

For example, here are two tables from University Town as reminders of what was achieved. These tables report the results on quality of expository writing, which was assessed by scoring sets of writing samples collected from students in fall 1992 and spring 1993. Particular attention was given to expository writing, which has proved to be so difficult to teach (Applebee and others 1990). The data were compared with district baseline results derived from comparisons of fall 1991 and spring 1992 writing and with the average gains indicated by the National Assessment of Writing Progress (Applebee and others 1990 and 1994) for the nation as a whole.

Table 7.1 compares the means for two periods (fall 1992 and spring 1993) for three dimensions of writing quality: Focus/Organization, Support, and Grammar/Mechanics. Altogether, 95 sets of samples, representing 95 students and approximately 20 percent of the district's fourth-grade population, were compared.

Effect sizes computed between fall and spring scores were for Focus, 2.18; for Support, 1.53; and for Grammar/Mechanics, 1.37. All these are several times the effect-sizes of the national sample and of the baseline gains determined from the 1991-92 analyses.

To illustrate the magnitude of the difference, table 7.2 compares the mean results for the spring fourth-grade assessment with the fall sixth-grade results.

The gains here indicate that, in the area of writing, it is possible to increase gains per year to several times the average gain, even in a district with a tradition of very high achievement.

In both of these examples—in settings with histories of low student achievement and high student achievement—the faculties found that their own attitudes and beliefs became part of the inquiry. In both cases, they found that they had not really believed their students could learn so much more effectively. And neither did the parents. In both settings, collective efficacy increased as faculties

T A B L E   7.1

MEAN GRADE 4 SCORES ON EXPOSITORY WRITING
FOR FALL 1992 AND SPRING 1993

	Dimensions		
Period	*Focus/Org*	*Support*	*Gram/Mech*
Fall			
Mean	1.6	2.2	2.11
SD	0.55	0.65	0.65
Spring			
Mean	2.8	3.2	3.0
SD	0.94	0.96	0.97

T A B L E   7.2

MEAN GRADE 4 SPRING 1993 SCORES ON EXPOSITORY
WRITING COMPARED WITH THE MEAN GRADE 6
SCORES FROM FALL 1992

	Dimensions		
	Focus/Org	*Support*	*Gram/Mech*
Grade 4 Spr			
Mean	2.8	3.2	3.0
SD	0.94	0.96	0.97
Grade 6 Fall			
Mean	2.11	2.90	2.87
SD	0.56	0.72	0.67

"proved" that their students could learn far more than they had been
expected to learn.

Serious inquiry often leads us beyond the information we are
accustomed to using. Faculties may begin their collective inquiry by
using existing vital-signs data such as grades and referrals, then
collect new data such as how often and how well students are
comprehending and composing. But the inquiry doesn't necessarily

stop with these behavioral data. At times, faculty members will want to collect data about how students feel: about student values, about how students feel about themselves as learners, about their sense of independence, and about their developing concepts of themselves as effective human beings. These perceptual and attitudinal data can enrich a faculty's perspective and understanding of student behaviors and of student responses to the learning opportunities provided.

HYPOTHESIS 4:
CONNECTING THE FACULTY TO THE KNOWLEDGE BASE ON TEACHING AND LEARNING WILL GENERATE MORE SUCCESSFUL INITIATIVES.

Not only has teaching lacked provisions for collective study of the learning environment, it has lacked provisions for study of the knowledge base that experientially and theoretically grounds our profession. Thus, many faculties have had to try to improve their schools without easy access to the accumulated knowledge relevant to their needs. Much to the benefit of all parties concerned with school improvement, the study of teaching, curriculum, and technology has a substantial knowledge base that can help faculties think about promising actions and possible solutions to problems (see Bloom 1984; Joyce and Weil 1996; Walberg 1990; Wang, Haertel, and Walberg 1993). In our modern information world, access can be provided easily.

This connection to the knowledge base of our profession and use of it as another source of information for collective inquiry can expand the possibilities for effective action, as faculty members locate efforts and perspectives that may not have been in their original frame of reference. For example, many Responsible Parties naturally seek for ways of motivating students to learn and, beginning their inquiry into that area, look for "motivational" programs. A broad look at the literature will reveal that there are teaching strategies and curricular approaches that have very large motivational effects, something that might not be found in a search for motivational programs alone.

A Brief Scenario: Moving Beyond What We Know The faculty and parents at Soquel Elementary School were working together to improve student writing from kindergarten through sixth grade. They had been dismayed as they looked at the number of students in grades 3 through 6 who were performing poorly in writing; they knew their students could do better.

Teachers and parents working together developed an action plan filled with exciting activities revolving around writing: A Write-Night Sleep-in, visits from renowned children's authors in the state, a family-night writing workshop, "Publication Boards" in each hall, Buzzy Bear stickers for papers, and surveys of students' and parents' attitudes about writing. Much faculty and parent energy went into conducting these activities.

At the same time, members of the Responsible Parties were seeking information from journals, textbooks on teaching composition, articles about what had worked in other schools, and so forth. They studied the resources they gathered, focusing on those that were directly related to improving the quality of student writing. They selected five resources for schoolwide study and reflection.

When the Soquel students produced writing samples again, there was an improvement in writing quality, but very little in proportion to the amount of energy the community had expended. By this time, the articles from the professional literature had been read, discussed, and debated during study-group meetings and even at a few parent/teacher meetings. As faculty members and parents reflected on the year's experiences and on their action plan, they realized that while they had done much to celebrate writing as a valuable activity, they had done nothing in terms of changes in instruction or curriculum. They began to design their 1993-94 action plan with an emphasis on instructional strategies that have a history of improving the quality of student writing.

HYPOTHESIS 5:

STAFF DEVELOPMENT, STRUCTURED AS AN INQUIRY INTO CURRICULUM AND INSTRUCTION, WILL PROVIDE SYNERGY AND RESULT IN INITIATIVES THAT HAVE GREATER STUDENT EFFECTS.

Staff development has to become a regular event, but not offered as a "Here is stuff that has been researched, so use it!" mode, but designed as an opening to new inquiries. For teachers to use the knowledge base to add to their repertoire of teaching strategies or to create different learning environments, they cannot simply find out that something "has worked" in some other setting. They have to develop the skill to use that information or strategy as they conduct disciplined inquiry into its effects on their students.

Consequently, the content of staff development—curriculum and instruction—must be organized so that as new practices are implemented the faculty can immediately and systematically study their effects. Models of teaching (Joyce and Showers 1995; Joyce and Weil 1996; Wang, Haertel, and Walberg 1993) are not static practices that one simply puts in place; they are models of learning that launch further study of the students and of how they learn.

HYPOTHESIS 6:

WORKING IN SMALL GROUPS WHERE MEMBERS ARE RESPONSIBLE FOR THEIR OWN LEARNING AND FOR HELPING ONE ANOTHER, NESTED WITHIN THE FACULTY AS A NURTURANT ORGANIZATIONAL UNIT, WILL INCREASE THE SENSE OF BELONGING THAT REDUCES ISOLATION, STRESS, AND FEELINGS OF ALIENATION.

A major dimension of schooling is creating caring communities for children. How to develop schools as organizations that nurture the professionals who work within them has received much less attention, despite the existence of a large body of literature on the stresses of teaching, the liabilities of "burning out," and the characteristics of "adult learners." Simply building closer professional communities, developing democratic interchange (legitimizing respectful and public adult interaction), and embedding the study of teaching into the workday can be hypothesized to have a considerable effect on professional ethos. And, as a structural process supporting these changes, inquiry can be argued for in terms of its effects on our collective mental health.

How can we develop schools as caring communities for those who work within their walls? Our assessment of the literature on organizations is that the caring dimension depends to a large extent on building organizations where many small groups—often composed of only three or four people—see themselves as not only working together to "get the job done," but also as having responsibility for seeing that one another receive support as they develop personally and professionally.

Thus, the larger school community both supports and is supported by small groups with at least two realms of responsibility: (1) inquiring into teaching and learning, and (2) supporting one another and the organization as a collaborative unit.

The University Town program illustrates many of the features of the school as a center of inquiry: embedded time for colleagueship; a system for shared-decision making; an information-rich, formative study environment; the study of research on curriculum and teaching; and a comprehensive staff development system that includes study groups.

INQUIRY NEVER ENDS

In essence, the focus of school renewal is on creating environments that promote the continuous examination of the process of education at all levels of the organization, so that knowledge-in-practice is continually expanding and so that specific, deliberate improvements can be launched and tested. For we—as individuals and as organizations—are never complete, never "finished." Classrooms, schools, and districts are social entities that, like the human spirit, require the challenge of growth not only to soar but to maintain themselves in optimum health.

APPENDIX

MEMBERSHIP OF THE GEORGIA LEAGUE OF PROFESSIONAL SCHOOLS, 1990-95

Year School Joined	Number of Schools Joining/Rejoining				
	1990-91	1991-92	1992-93	1993-94	1994-95
1990-91	24	22	22	19	18
1991-92		21	18	17	17
1992-93			20	18	16
1993-94					
1994-95					9
Total Number of Schools Each Year	24	43	60	54	60

TABLE A-2

DEMOGRAPHICS OF FOURTH-YEAR SCHOOLS (19), GEORGIA LEAGUE OF PROFESSIONAL SCHOOLS MARCH 1994

LEVEL	LOCATION	STUDENT POPULATION	%FREE/ REDUCED LUNCHES	%MINORITY
Elementary	Rural	164	35%	24%
Elementary	Rural	355	51%	11%
Elementary	Rural	376	53%	26%
Elementary	Suburban	380	17%	11%
Elementary	Suburban	530	39%	99%
Elementary	Urban	580	23%	28%
Elementary	Urban	650	73%	94%
Elementary	Suburban	730	5%	10%
Elementary	Suburban	900	4%	4%
Elementary	Rural	927	45%	1%
Elementary	Suburban	950	25%	10%
Elementary	Suburban	1042	21%	28%
Elementary	Suburban	1135	25%	40%
Middle	Suburban	802	6%	10%
Middle	Suburban	855	15%	7%
Middle	Suburban	1017	10%	25%
High	Rural	393	52%	45%
High	Suburban	1200	8%	10%
High	Suburban	1920	1%	7%

T A B L E   A-3

DEMOGRAPHICS OF THIRD-YEAR SCHOOLS (17), GEORGIA LEAGUE OF PROFESSIONAL SCHOOLS MARCH 1994

LEVEL	LOCATION	STUDENT POPULATION	%FREE/ REDUCED LUNCHES	%MINORITY
Elementary	Urban	492	63%	58%
Elementary	Rural	520	53%	6%
Elementary (K-1)	Rural	535	64%	45%
Elementary	Rural	570	29%	23%
Elementary	Rural	575	33%	4%
Elementary	Suburban	587	8%	2%
Elementary	Suburban	604	6%	9%
Elementary (K-3)	Rural	605	49%	39%
Elementary	Urban	616	90%	98%
Elementary	Suburban (City)	663	79%	73%
Elementary	Suburban	915	22%	22%
Middle	Urban	618	90%	70%
High	Rural	1218	35%	39%
High	Suburban	1300	2%	6%
High	Urban	1363	33%	50%
High	Urban	1400	54%	51%
High	Urban	2200	28%	59%

TABLE A-4

DEMOGRAPHICS OF SECOND-YEAR SCHOOLS (18),
GEORGIA LEAGUE OF PROFESSIONAL SCHOOLS
MARCH 1994

LEVEL	*LOCATION*	*STUDENT POPULATION*	*%FREE/ REDUCED LUNCHES*	*%MINORITY*
Elementary	Suburban	190	60%	3%
Elementary	Rural	445	40%	30%
Elementary	Rural	500	60%	45%
Elementary	Rural	673	15%	2%
Elementary	Suburban	689	9%	9%
Elementary	Suburban	710	5%	2%
Elementary	Rural (City)	748	48%	30%
Elementary	Suburban	824	20%	10%
Elementary	Rural	1091	61%	44%
Middle	Suburban	610	17%	9%
Middle	Rural	710	31%	5%
Middle	Rural (City)	720	70%	77%
Middle	Suburban	890	23%	11%
Middle	Suburban	965	11%	8%
Middle	Suburban	1748		6%
High	Suburban	480	8%	3%
High	Urban	1328	31%	63%
High	Rural	1450	37%	30%

T A B L E A-5				

LEAGUE OF PROFESSIONAL SCHOOLS
USE OF INFORMATION-RETRIEVAL SYSTEM BY
FOURTH-YEAR SCHOOLS—NUMBER OF SCHOOLS
MAKING REQUESTS
MARCH 1994

LEVEL	*LOCATION*	*STUDENT POPULATION*	*NO. REQUESTS MADE* Feb 90-Feb 93	*NO. REQUESTS MADE* Mar 93-Feb 94
Elementary	Rural	164	0	3
Elementary	Rural	355	16	1
Elementary	Rural	376	6	4
Elementary	Suburban	380	8	9
Elementary	Suburban	530	4	0
Elementary	Urban	580	4	6
Elementary	Urban	650	8	0
Elementary	Suburban	730	3	7
Elementary	Suburban	900	7	1
Elementary	Rural	927	14	8
Elementary	Suburban	950	2	0
Elementary	Suburban	1042	17	6
Elementary	Suburban	1135	6	1
Middle	Suburban	802	1	1
Middle	Suburban	855	3	6
Middle	Suburban	1017	6	2
High	Rural	393	2	0
High	Suburban	1200	6	3
High	Suburban	1920	4	0

TOTAL NUMBER OF SCHOOLS MAKING REQUESTS FOR 1993-94: 14
(In 1990, 24 schools could have made requests; in 1991 and 1992, 22 schools could have made requests; in 1993, 19 schools could have made requests.)

T A B L E A-6

LEAGUE OF PROFESSIONAL SCHOOLS
USE OF INFORMATION-RETRIEVAL SYSTEM BY THIRD-YEAR
SCHOOLS—NUMBER OF SCHOOLS MAKING REQUESTS
MARCH 1994

LEVEL	LOCATION	STUDENT POPULATION	NO. REQUESTS MADE Mar 91-Feb 93	NO. REQUESTS MADE Mar 93-Feb 94
Elementary	Urban	492	0	2
Elementary	Rural	520	4	1
Elementary (K-1)	Rural	535	7	1
Elementary	Rural	570	9	0
Elementary	Rural	575	17	1
Elementary	Suburban	587	7	0
Elementary	Suburban	604	3	0
Elementary (K-3)	Rural	605	5	1
Elementary	Urban	616	7	1
Elementary	Suburban (City)	663	5	3
Elementary	Suburban	915	5	0
Middle	Urban	618	1	0
High	Rural	1218	7	0
High	Suburban	1300	5	2
High	Urban	1363	2	2
High	Urban	1400	1	20
High	Urban	2200	0	18

TOTAL NUMBER OF SCHOOLS MAKING REQUESTS FOR 1993-94: 11
(In 1991, 21 schools could have made requests; in 1992, 18 schools could have made requests; in 1993, 17 schools could have made requests.)

T A B L E   A-7

LEAGUE OF PROFESSIONAL SCHOOLS
USE OF INFORMATION-RETRIEVAL SYSTEM BY
SECOND-YEAR SCHOOLS—NUMBER OF SCHOOLS
MAKING REQUESTS
MARCH 1994

LEVEL	LOCATION	STUDENT POPULATION	NO. REQUESTS MADE Mar 92-Feb 93	NO. REQUESTS MADE Mar 93-Feb 94
Elementary	Suburban	190	0	3
Elementary	Rural	445	3	1
Elementary	Rural	500	9	4
Elementary	Rural	673	0	8
Elementary	Suburban	689	0	4
Elementary	Suburban	710	6	4
Elementary	Rural (City)	748	1	2
Elementary	Suburban	824	0	10
Elementary	Rural	1091	2	3
Middle	Suburban	610	0	2
Middle	Rural	634	1	0
Middle	Rural (City)	720	2	0
Middle	Suburban	890	1	2
Middle	Suburban	965	2	1
Middle	Suburban	1748	0	1
High	Urban	1328	1	0
High	Rural	1450	1	3

TOTAL NUMBER OF SCHOOLS MAKING REQUESTS FOR 1993-94: 14
(In 1992, 20 schools could have made requests; in 1993, 18 schools could have made requests.)

BIBLIOGRAPHY

Many of the items in this bibliography are indexed in ERIC's monthly catalog *Resources in Education* (*RIE*). Reports in *RIE* are indicated by an "ED" number. Journal articles, indexed in ERIC's companion catalog, *Current Index to Journals in Education,* are indicated by an "EJ" number.

Most items with an ED number are available from ERIC Document Reproduction Service (EDRS), 7420 Fullerton Rd., Suite 110, Springfield, VA 22153-2852.

To order from EDRS, specify the ED number, type of reproduction desired—microfiche (MF) or paper copy (PC), and number of copies. Add postage to the cost of all orders and include check or money order payable to EDRS. For credit card orders, call 1-800-443-3742.

Adler, M.J. (1982). *The paidea proposal: An educational manifesto.* New York: Macmillan.

Ainscow, M., Hopkins, D., Southworth, G., & West, M. (1994). *Creating the conditions for school improvement.* London: David Fulton Publishers.

Applebee, A., Langer, J., Jenkins, L., Mullis, I., & Foertsch, M. (1990). *Learning to write in our nation's schools*: *Instruction and achievement in 1988 at grades 4, 8, and 12.* Princeton, New Jersey: National Assessment of Educational Progress. ED 318 038.

Applebee, A. N., Langer, J. A., Mullis, I. V. S., Latham, A.S., & Gentile, C.A. (1994). *NAEP 1992 writing report card.* Washington, D.C.: Prepared by Educational Testing Service under contract with the National Center for Education Statistics for the Office of Educational Research and Improvement, U.S. Department of Education.

Baldridge, V. & Deal, T. E. (1983). *The dynamics of organizational change in education.* Berkeley: McCutchan.

Barth, R. (1990). *Improving schools from within.* San Francisco: Jossey-Bass Publishers.

Barth, R.S. (1991). Restructuring schools: Some questions for teachers and principals. *Phi Delta Kappan, 73* (2), 123-128. EJ 432 758.

Becker, W. C. (1977). Teaching reading and language to the disadvantaged—What we have learned from field research. *Harvard Educational Review, 47*, 518-543.

Becker, W., & Carnine, D. (1980). Direct instruction: An effective approach for educational intervention with the disadvantaged and low performers. In B. Lahey and A. Kazdin (Eds.), *Advances in child clinical psychology*, pp. 429-473. New York: Plenum.

Becker, W., & Gersten, R. (1982). A followup of Follow Through: The later effects of the direct instruction model on children in fifth and sixth grades. *American Educational Research Journal, 19* (1), 75-92. EJ 271 993.

Bennis, W. G. (1989). *Why leaders can't lead. The Unconscious Conspiracy Continues*. San Francisco: Jossey-Bass. ED 314 991.

Berman, P., & Gjelten, T. (1983). *Improving school improvement*. Berkeley: Berman, Weiler Associates.

Beyer, B. (1988). *Developing a thinking skills program*. Boston: Allyn Bacon.

Block, J. W., & Anderson, L. W. (1975). *Mastery learning in classrooms*. New York: Macmillan.

Bloom, B.S. (1984). The 2 sigma problem: The search for group instruction as effective as one-to-one tutoring. *Educational Researcher, 13* (6), 4-16. EJ 303 699.

Bonstingl, J.J. (1992). *Schools of quality: An introduction to total quality management in education*. Alexandria, VA: Association for Supervision and Curriculum Development. ED 362 937.

Butler-Kisber L. (1993). Action research: Incorporating the voices of children. Paper presented at the annual meeting of the American Educational Research Association, Atlanta. ED 361 375.

Calhoun, E. F. (1991). A wide-angle lens: How to increase the variety, collection, and use of data for school improvement. Paper presented at the annual meeting of the American Educational Research Association, Chicago. ED 335 797.

Calhoun, E. F. (1992). A status report on action research in the League of Professional Schools. Paper presented at the annual meeting of the American Educational Research Association, San Francisco.

Calhoun, E.F. (1993). Action research: Three approaches. *Educational Leadership, 51*(2), 62-65. EJ 470 572.

Calhoun, E.F. (1994). *How to use action research in the self-renewing school*. Alexandria, VA: ASCD. ED 370 205.

Calhoun, E.F., & Allen, L. (1994). Results of schoolwide action research in the League of Professional Schools. Paper presented at the annual meeting of the American Educational Research Association, New Orleans. ED 370 969.

Calhoun, E. F., & Glickman, C.D. (1993). Issues and Dilemmas of action research in the League of Professional Schools. Paper presented at the annual meeting of the American Educational Research Association, Atlanta.

Carran, N. (1993). The Teacher Satisfaction and Productivity Interview. Ames, IA: Ames Community Schools.

Chall, J.S. (1983). *Stages of reading development.* New York: McGraw-Hill.

Conant, J.B. (1961). *Slums and suburbs.* New York: McGraw-Hill.

Corey, S. M. (1949). Curriculum development through action research. *Educational Leadership, 7*(3), 147-153.

Corey, S. M. (1953). *Action research to improve school practices.* New York: Teachers College Press.

Cuban, L. (1990). Reforming again, again, and again. *Educational Researcher, 19* (1), 3-13. EJ 408 024.

David, J. L. (1990). Restructuring: Increased autonomy and changing roles. Invited address presented at the annual meeting of the American Educational Research Association, Boston.

David, J. L. (1991). What it takes to restructure education. *Educational Leadership, 48*(8), 11-15. EJ 425 600.

David, J. L., & Peterson, S.M. (1984). Can schools improve themselves? A study of school-based improvement programs. Palo Alto: Bay Area Research Group. ED 262 119.

Deal, T. E. (1993). The culture of the school. In M. Sashkin & H. Walberg (Ed.), *Educational leadership and school culture.* San Pablo, Berkeley: McCutchan.

Drucker, P.F. (1985). *Innovation and entrepreneurship: Practice and principles.* New York: Harper and Row.

Drucker, P.F. (1989). *The new realities.* New York: Harper & Row.

Eisner, E. W. (1993). Forms of understanding and the future of educational research. *Educational Researcher, 22*(7), 5.

Elliott, J. (1991). *Action research for educational change.* Bristol, PA: Open University Press.

Evans, M., & Hopkins, D. (1988). School climate and the psychological state of the individual teacher as factors affecting the use of educational ideas following an inservice course. *British Educational Research Journal, 14* (3), 211-230. EJ 384 678.

Fullan, M. G. (1982). *The meaning of educational change.* New York: Teachers College Press.

Fullan, M. G. (1992). *Successful school improvement. The implementation perspective and beyond.* Buckingham, UK: Open University Press. ED 377 593.

Fullan, M. G. (1993). *Change forces.* London: The Falmer Press.

Fullan, M. G., & Miles, M. B. (1992). Getting reform right: What works and what doesn't. *Phi Delta Kappan, 73* (10), 744-52. EJ 445 727.

Fullan, M.G., & Pomfret, A. (1977). Research on curriculum and instruction implementation. *Review of Educational Research, 47*(1), 335-397.

Fullan, M.G., and S. Steigelbauer. (1991). *The new meaning of educational change.* New York: Teachers College Press. ED 354 588.

Gagne, R. (1965). *The conditions of learning.* New York: Holt, Rinehart, and Winston.

Gagne, R. (1975). *Essentials of learning for instruction.* New York: Holt, Rinehart, and Winston.

Glickman, C. D. (1985). *Supervision of instruction: A developmental approach.* Boston: Allyn and Bacon. ED 283 286.

Glickman, C. D. (1993). *Renewing America's schools: A guide for school-based action.* San Francisco: Jossey-Bass. ED 364 963.

Glickman, C. D., & Allen, L. (Eds.). (1991). *Lessons from the field: Renewing schools through shared governance and action research.* Athens, GA: Program for School Improvement, University of Georgia.

Glickman, C.D., Allen, L., & Lunsford, B.F. (1994). Factors affecting school change. *Journal of Staff Development, 15* (3), pp. 37-41. EJ 490 250.

Goodlad, J. I. (1984). *A place called school. Prospects for the future.* New York: McGraw-Hill. ED 236 137.

Goodlad, J.I., & Klein, M.F. (1970). *Looking behind the classroom door.* Worthington, OH: Charles E. Jones.

Hall, G.E., & Hord, S.M. (1987). *Change in schools: Facilitating the process.* New York: State University of New York. ED 332 261.

Hall, G. & Loucks, S. (1977). A developmental model for determining whether the treatment is actually implemented. *American Educational Research Journal, 14* (3), 263-276.

Hallinger, P., & Murphy, J. (1985). Assessing the instructional management behavior of principals. *Elementary School Journal, 86* (2), 217-247. EJ 328 595.

Havelock, R.G., Guskin, A., Frohman, M., Havelock, M., Hill, M., & Huber, J. (1969). *Planning for innovation through dissemination and utilization of knowledge.* Ann Arbor, MI: Institute for Social Research.

Heller, M.F. (1991). *Reading-writing connections: From theory to practice.* New York: Longman.

Hensley, F., Calhoun, E. F., & Glickman, C. D. (1992). Results from site-based, action research schools: What has been accomplished? What are the next steps? Paper presented at the annual meeting of the American Educational Research Association, San Francisco.

Hillocks, G. (1987). Synthesis of research on teaching writing. *Educational Leadership, 44* (8), 71-76, 78, 80-82. EJ 353 889.

Hollingsworth, S., & Sockett, H. (Eds.) (1994). *Teacher research and educational reform: The ninety-third yearbook of the National Society for the Study of Education.* Chicago: University of Chicago Press.

Huberman, A.M. (1992). Successful school improvement: Reflections and observations. (Critical introduction to M. G. Fullan (1992), *Successful school improvement.*)

Huberman, A. M., & Miles, M. B. (1986). Rethinking the quest for school improvement: Some findings from the DESSI study. In Ann Lieberman (Ed.), *Rethinking school improvement: Research, craft, and concept.* New York: Teachers College Press. EJ 309 292.

Huberman, A. M., & Miles, M. B. (1984). *Innovation up close.* New York: Praeger. ED 240 716.

Journal of Staff Development. (1993). *14* (3), 2-8.

Joyce, B. (Ed.), (1990). *Changing school culture through staff development.* The 1990 Yearbook of the Association for Supervision and Curriculum Development. Alexandria, Va.: The Association for Supervision and Curriculum Development. ED 315 919.

Joyce, B.R. (1991). The doors to school improvement. *Educational Leadership, 48* (8), 59-62. EJ 425 610.

Joyce, B.R. (1992). Cooperative learning and staff development: Teaching the method with the method. *Cooperative Learning, 12* (2), 10-13.

Joyce, B., Bush, R., & McKibbin, M. (1982). *The California staff development study: The January 1982 report.* Palo Alto: Booksend Laboratories.

Joyce, B., & Calhoun, E. (1995). School renewal: An inquiry not a formula. *Educational Leadership, 52* (7), 51-55. EJ 502 912.

Joyce, B., Calhoun, E., Halliburton, C., Simser, J., Rust, D. & Carran, N. (1994). The Ames Community Schools staff development program. Paper presented at the annual meeting of the Association for Supervision and Curriculum Development, Chicago.

Joyce, B., Hersh, R., & McKibbin, M. (1983). *The structure of school improvement.* New York: Longman. ED 228 233.

Joyce, B.R., McKibbin, M., & Bush, R. (1983). The seasons of professional life: The growth states of teachers. Paper presented at the annual meeting of the American Education Research Association, Montreal, Canada.

Joyce, B., Murphy, C., Showers, B., & Murphy, J. (1989). School renewal as cultural change. *Educational Leadership, 47* (3), 70-77. EJ 398 956.

Joyce, B., & Showers, B. (1980). Improving inservice training: The messages of research. *Educational Leadership, 37* (5), 379-385.

Joyce, B., & Showers, B. (1982). The coaching of teaching. *Educational Leadership, 40* (1), 4-8, 10. EJ 268 889.

Joyce, B., & Showers, B. (1983). *Power in staff development through research on training.* Washington: Association for Supervision and Curriculum Development. ED 240 667.

Joyce, B., and Showers, B. (1988). *Student achievement through staff development.* White Plains, NY: Longman. ED 283 817.

Joyce, B., & Showers, B. (1995). *Student achievement through staff development*. (2nd ed.). White Plains, NY: Longman.

Joyce, B., Showers, B., & Rolheiser-Bennett, C. (1987). Staff development and student learning: A synthesis of research on models of teaching. *Educational Leadership, 45* (2), 11-23. EJ 362 222.

Joyce, B., & Weil, M. (1986). *Models of teaching* (3rd ed.). Englewood Cliffs, NJ: Prentice-Hall.

Joyce, B., & Weil, M. (1996). *Models of teaching* (5th ed.). Boston: Allyn & Bacon.

Joyce, B., Weil, M., & Showers, B. (1992). *Models of teaching* (4th ed.). Boston: Allyn & Bacon.

Joyce, B., & Wolf, J. (1992). Operation just read and write: Toward a literate society. Paper presented at the annual meeting of the Association for Supervision and Curriculum Development, New Orleans.

Joyce, B., Wolf, J., & Calhoun, E. (1993). *The self-renewing school*. Alexandria: Association for Supervision and Curriculum Development. ED 362 946.

Kozol, J. (1967). *Death at an early age: The destruction of the hearts and minds of Negro children in the Boston public schools*. Boston: Houghton Mifflin.

Kozol, J. (1992). *Savage inequalities. Children in America's Schools*. New York: Harper Collins. ED 365 035.

Levine, D.U. (1991). Creating effective schools: Findings and implications from research and practice. *Phi Delta Kappan, 72* (5), 389-393. EJ 419 911.

Lewin, K. (1947). Group decisions and social change. In T. M. Newcomb & E. L. Hartley (Eds.), *Readings in social psychology*. New York: Henry Holt.

Lewin, K. (1946). *Resolving social conflicts: Selected papers on group dynamics*. New York: Harper and Row.

Little, J.W. (1982). Norms of collegiality and experimentation: Workplace conditions of school success. *American Educational Research Journal, 19*(3), 325-40. EJ 275 511.

Little, J.W. (1990). The persistence of privacy: Autonomy and initiative in teachers' professional relations. *Teachers College Record, 91*(4), 509-536. EJ 412 496.

Lortie, D. (1975). *Schoolteacher*. Chicago: University of Chicago Press.

Louis, K., & Miles, M. B. (1990). *Improving the urban high school: What Works and Why*. New York: Teachers College Press. ED 327 623.

Madden, N.A., Slavin, R.E., Karweit, N.L., Dolan, L.J., & Wasik, B.A. (1993). Success For All: Longitudinal effects of a restructuring program for inner-city elementary schools. *American Educational Research Journal, 30*(1), 123-148. EJ 463 408.

Maehr, R., & Buck, R. (1993). Transforming school culture. In M. Sashkin & H. Walberg (Eds.), *Educational leadership and school culture*. San Pablo, Berkeley: McCutchan. ED 367 056.

McKibbin, M., & Joyce, B. (1980). Psychological states and staff development. *Theory into Practice, 19* (4), 248-255.

Miles, M. B. (1992). 40 years of change in schools: Some personal reflections. Paper presented at the annual meeting of the American Educational Research Association, San Francisco.

Muncey, D. (1994). Individual and schoolwide change in eight Coalition Schools: Findings from a longitudinal ethnographic study. Paper presented at the annual meeting of the American Educational Research Association, New Orleans.

Muncey, D. E., & McQuillan, P. J. (1993). Preliminary findings from a five-year study of the Coalition of Essential Schools. *Phi Delta Kappan, 74*(6), 486-489. EJ 457 284.

Murphy, J., & Hallinger, P. (Eds.). (1993). *Restructuring schooling: Learning from ongoing efforts.* Newbury Park, CA: Corwin Press. ED 357 437.

Mutchler, Sue E., & Duttweiler, Patricia C. (1990). Implementing shared decision making in school-based management: Barriers to changing traditional behavior. Paper presented at the annual meeting of the American Educational Research Association, Boston.

Myers, M. (1985). *The teacher-researcher: How to study writing in the classroom.* Urbana: The National Council of Teachers of English. ED 261 394.

National Assessment of Educational Progress (NAEP). (1992). *The reading report card for the nation and the states.* Washington, D.C.: National Center for Educational Statistics. U.S. Department of Education.

Passow, A.H. (Ed.). (1963). *Education in depressed areas.* New York: Teachers College.

Prestine, N. A. (1992). Benchmarks of change: Assessing essential school restructuring efforts. *Education Evaluation and Policy Analysis 15* (3), 298-319. EJ 471 908.

Quellmalz, E.S., and Burry, J. (1983). Analytic scales for assessing students' expository and narrative writing skills. Los Angeles: Center for The Study of Evaluation, UCLA Graduate School of Education. (CSE Resource Paper No. 5)*Review of Educational Research.* (1993). *63* (3). ED 277 006.

Rollow, S. G., & Bryk, A. S. (1993). Catalyzing professional community in a school reform left behind. Paper presented at the annual meeting of the American Educational Research Association, Atlanta.

Rosenholtz, S.J. (1989). *Teachers' workplace: The social organization of schools.* White Plains, NY: Longman.

Sarason, S. (1982). *The culture of the school and the problems of change* (2nd ed.). Boston: Allyn and Bacon.

Sarason, S. (1990). *The predictable failure of school reform: Can we change the course before it's too late?* San Francisco: Jossey-Bass.

Schaefer, R. J. (1967). *The school as a center of inquiry.* New York: Harper and Row.

Senge, P. M. (1990). *The fifth discipline: The art and practice of the learning organization.* New York: Doubleday.

Sergiovanni, T.J. (1994). *Building community in schools.* San Francisco: Jossey-Bass. ED 364 962.

Sharan, S. (Ed.) (1990). *Cooperative learning: Theory and research.* New York: Praeger.

Sharan, S., & Hertz-Lazarowitz, R. (1982). Effects of an instructional change program on teachers' behaviors, attitudes, and perceptions. *The Journal of Applied Behavioral Science, 18* (2), 185-201.

Sharan, S., & Hertz-Lazarowitz, R. (1988). *Language and learning in the cooperative classroom.* New York: Springer-Verlag.

Showers, B. (1989). School improvement through staff development: Levels of implementation and impact on student achievement. Paper presented at the International Conference on "School-Based Innovations: Looking Forward to the 1990's," Hong Kong.

Sirotnik, K. (1983). What you see is what you get: Consistency, persistence, and mediocrity in classrooms. *Harvard Educational Review, 53* (1), 16-31. EJ 275 754.

Sirotnik, K. A. (1987). Evaluation in the ecology of schooling. In J.I. Goodlad (Ed.), *The Ecology of school renewal: The eighty-sixth yearbook of the National Society for the Study of Education.* Chicago: The University of Chicago Press.

Sizer, T. R. (1985). *Horace's compromise.* Boston: Houghton-Mifflin. ED 264 171.

Sizer, T. R. (1992). *Horace's school: Redesigning the American high school.* Boston: Houghton Mifflin.

Slavin, R. E., & Madden, N. A. (1995). Success for All: Creating schools and classrooms where all children can read. In J. Oakes and K. H. Quartz (Eds.), *Creating new* educational communities: Ninety-fourth yearbook of the National Society for the *Study of Education.*

Slavin, R. E., Madden, N. A., Karweit, N., Livermon, B. J., & Dolan, L. (1990). Success For All: First-year outcomes of a comprehensive plan for reforming urban education. *American Educational Research Journal, 27*(2), 255-278. EJ 414 291.

Smith, W. E. (1993). Teachers' perceptions of role change through shared decision making: A two year case study. Paper presented at the annual meeting of the American Educational Research Association, Atlanta.

Sparks, D. (1993). Insights on school improvement: An interview with Larry Lezotte. *Journal of staff development, 14*(3), 18-21. EJ 482 525.

Sparks, D., & Loucks-Horsley, S. (1992). *Five models of staff development for teachers. Journal of Staff Development 10* (4), 40-57. EJ 414 183.

Stiegelbauer, S., & Anderson, S. (1992) Seven years later: Revisiting a restructured school in Northern Ontario. Paper presented at the annual meeting of the American Educational Research Association, San Francisco. ED 347 686.

Strike, K. A. (1993). Professionalism, democracy, and discursive communities: Normative reflections on restructuring. *American Educational Research Journal, 30*(2), 255-275. EJ 466 287.

Walberg, H. J. (1990). Productive teaching and instruction: Assessing the knowledge base. *Phi Delta Kappan,* 71 (6), 470-78.

Wallace, J., & Wildy, H. (1993). Pioneering School Change: Lessons from a case study of school site restructuring. Paper presented at the annual meeting of the American Educational Research Association, Atlanta.

Wallace, R. C., Lemahieu, P. G., & Bickel, W. E. (1990). The Pittsburgh experience: Achieving commitment to comprehensive staff development. In B. Joyce (Ed.), *Changing school culture through staff development.* Alexandria: Association for Supervision and Curriculum Development.

Waller, W. (1965). *The sociology of teaching.* New York: Wiley. (Originally published in 1932.)

Wang, M., Haertel, G., & Walberg, H. (1993). Toward a knowledge base for school learning. *Review of Educational Research, 63* (3), 249-294.

Weick, K.E. (1976). Educational organizations as loosely coupled systems. *Administrative Science Quarterly, 21,* 1-19.

CONTRIBUTORS

Lew Allen is Director of Outreach, PSI League of Professional Schools, The University of Georgia, Athens, Georgia.

Emily Calhoun is Director of The Phoenix Alliance, Saint Simons Island, Georgia.

Nina Carran is Assistant Superintendent of Ames Community Schools, Ames, Iowa.

Cal Halliburton is a Teacher at Ames Middle School, Ames, Iowa.

Henry Izumizaki is Program Officer, The Commission for Positive Change, Oakland, California.

Bruce Joyce is Director of Booksend Laboratories, Pauma Valley, California.

Carlene Murphy is an Educational Consultant in Augusta, Georgia.

Dallas Rust is Principal of Roosevelt Elementary School, Ames, Iowa.

Beverly Showers is an Educational Consultant in Aptos, California.

Jay Simser is a Teacher at Edwards Elementary School, Ames, Iowa.

James Wolf is Director of Synergistic Schools, Sugar Land, Texas.

REVIEWERS

The following persons made detailed reviews of the manuscript and tried to set us right.

Kitty Blumsack, Coordinator, School Improvement Training Unit, Rockville, Maryland.

Ron Brandt, Executive Editor, Association for Supervision and Curriculum Development, Alexandria, Virginia.

Gordon Cawelti, Executive Director, Alliance for Curriculum Reform, Arlington, Virginia.

Joy Coleman, Principal, Ballard Elementary School, Brunswick, Georgia.

Sandee Crowther, Director of Evaluation and Standards, Lawrence Public Schools, Lawrence, Kansas.

Jan Fisher, Staff Developer, Newport/Mesa Unified School District, Newport Beach, California.

Russell Gersten, Professor of Education, College of Education, University of Oregon, Eugene, Oregon.

Carolyn Jons, President, Iowa School Boards Association and a member of the Board in Ames, Iowa.

Chris Jurenka, Principal, Kaiser Elementary School, Costa Mesa, California.

Joellen Killion, Staff Development Specialist, Staff Development Training Center, Northglenn, Colorado.

Pamela Lewis, Assistant Superintendent, Glynn County Schools, Brunswick, Georgia.

Shelly Smith, Consultant, First District Regional Educational Service Agency, Vidallia, Georgia.

Stuart Smith, Associate Director, ERIC Clearinghouse on Educational Management, University of Oregon, Eugene, Oregon.

Dennis Sparks, Executive Director, National Staff Development Council, Dearborn, Michigan.